CHRISTIANIT

DISRAELI; POVERTY AND WEALTH

Christianity, Poverty and Wealth

The findings of 'Project 21'

Michael Taylor

WCC Publications

SPCK

Published in Great Britain in 2003 by
Society for Promoting Christian Knowledge
Holy Trinity Church
Marylebone Road
London NW1 4DU
and in Switzerland by
WCC Publications, World Council of Churches
150 route de Ferney, P.O. Box 2100
1211 Geneva 2, Switzerland

British Library Cataloguing-in-Publication Data
A catalogue record for this book is available from the British Library

SPCK ISBN 0–281–05547–5
WCC ISBN 2–8254–1374–7

1 3 5 7 9 10 8 6 4 2

Typeset by Wilmaset Ltd, Birkenhead, Wirral
Printed in Great Britain by
Antony Rowe, Chippenham, Wiltshire

dedicated to
Innocent Kaseke
of Christian Care, Zimbabwe
who shared in this project
until his early death in 2001

CONTENTS

Foreword   ix

Preface   xiii

'2015 Millennium Goals' for the Churches – A Call to Action   xiv

1   Poverty and Wealth   1
2   Causes   12
3   The Teaching of the Churches   25
4   Overcoming Poverty   37
5   The Actions of the Churches   49
6   Recommendations   58
7   Combating Poverty and Greed   68
8   The Story of 'Project 21'   81

    Appendix – List of Participants   92

    Notes   94

    Index   97

FOREWORD

Fighting poverty has moved back into the centre of the international agenda after having been over-shadowed for some time by a primary emphasis on policies of structural adjustment and incentives for growth. In preparation for the UN Special Session on Social Development (Geneva 2000) and the Millennium Summit of the United Nations, the target of reducing poverty to half by the year 2015 has been adopted as a benchmark by all international organizations involved in social development. Recent meetings, like the UN conference at Monterrey on Financing for Development, have given rise to new doubts whether there is the political will to work towards reaching these goals.

The Christian churches were involved in the struggle against poverty long before the proclamation of the first development decade. Traditionally, the churches' response has been characterized by the work of charity without challenging the political, social and economic structures that are the root causes of poverty. Over the last more than 30 years the ecumenical community of churches has become more and more involved in the development debate. It has sought to spell out what it means to be a 'church in solidarity with the poor'. It has sponsored studies on 'patterns of poverty' and engaged in advocacy programmes challenging the root causes of poverty.

Even though the biblical tradition is much more explicit about excessive wealth and the ways it can corrupt human community, the Christian churches have been reluctant to address the ethical and spiritual issues related to wealth. In some traditions wealth has been regarded as a sign of divine blessing, often with the implication that the poor are to blame for their poverty. Today, these views are being defended by churches that proclaim a 'prosperity gospel'. At the same time, however, ecumenical discussion has begun to focus attention on the hidden links between poverty and wealth. Just as it has become common to speak of a 'poverty line' there should be a limit beyond which the accumulation of wealth becomes greed and is no longer ethically and socially acceptable. This would mean calling for an 'economy of enough'.

The geo-political changes during the last decade of the twentieth century and the accelerating process of economic globalization have obliged the churches and ecumenical organizations to rethink the principles, objectives and methodologies guiding their participation in development. The project 'Discerning the Way Together', sponsored in the years after 1993 by the World Council of Churches with the participation of four Northern church-related development agencies and four networks of Southern partners, reinforced the need for further critical reflection.

Here is the origin of the initiative leading to the present publication. It began in 1997 when the World Council of Churches and its ecumenical partners in the Association of World Council of Churches related Development Organisations in Europe (APRODEV) initiated a process of case studies in order to gain a better understanding of how churches, agencies and ecumenical organizations could respond more effectively to poverty in the twenty-first century. Eventually 19 country studies were commissioned with a clear priority given to countries in the Southern hemisphere and complemented by five issue studies. All studies followed a similar methodology. The objective was to give voice to the people who are exposed to poverty and not to add to the plethora of academic research publications or political action programmes. The outcome of 'Project 21' was intended to be informative and also challenging with a clear emphasis on the role of the churches in the broader struggles against poverty.

The story of 'Project 21' is told in the last chapter of this book. The main body of the publication represents a summary of the findings of the 24 case studies. The structure is clear and self-explanatory with each chapter being introduced with an epigraph highlighting the main contents. Much of the information emerging from the case studies is not new or surprising for those who are familiar with the ecumenical development debate. However, the book makes a specific contribution by including wealth and greed alongside poverty in its investigation, by placing the churches into the wider ('ecumenical') context of civil society, and by arguing that a global advocacy alliance should be formed for eradicating poverty.

Considering strategies for stimulating effective action by the churches, those responsible for 'Project 21' developed the proposal to issue at regular intervals a 'World Church Report on Poverty and Wealth' to complement the development reports by the United Nations Development Programme (UNDP) and the World Bank. Instead of tables and statistics this church report should reflect the specific experiences of people in local contexts. Published every 3–5 years, the report would allow for an assessment of how far the churches have been able to meet the targets set. And in fact, the present book is presented as a 'prototype' of a future World Church

Report and includes a list of ten goals for the churches' action until the year 2015 (see pp. xiv and 78). These goals are an attempt to develop a clear strategy for combating poverty and greed.

The project has set a very ambitious goal for itself. It is unavoidable that a report of this kind will leave many gaps and that its conceptual and methodological assumptions may be open to challenge. However, in spite of the disclaimers included in the report itself, this publication represents a very significant effort to arrive at a common framework of interpretation which is the very condition for building a global alliance in the struggle against poverty. This book invites critical discussion in order to learn from such reactions how to improve the conceptual framework of a World Church Report on Poverty and Wealth.

KONRAD RAISER
General Secretary, World Council of Churches
May 2002

PREFACE

The dawn of the twenty-first century seemed an appropriate moment to ask whether churches were bringing good news to the poor and going about it in the right way. Over 24 countries were part of this study project initiated by the Association of World Council of Churches related Development Organisations in Europe (APRODEV) in collaboration with the World Council of Churches and nicknamed 'Project 21'. Twenty-four case studies were written. Nineteen of them were based on countries (Bangladesh, Chile, China (Hong Kong), Colombia, Fiji, Germany, Ghana, India, Jamaica, Malaysia, Namibia, Nicaragua, Palestine, Philippines, Russia, South Africa, South Korea, Uganda, West Indies). Five of them focused on particular subjects (the labour movement, liturgy, transnational corporations, the especially disadvantaged position of women, the United Nations). In writing them, rich and poor, high and low, activist and official, lay and expert were asked for their views. All the case studies are available on the Project's website < http://www.aprodev.net >.

The Project involved several meetings of the case study writers and a major Colloquium in New Delhi in November 2000 which produced an interim 'Working Document'. The full story of the Project is told in chapter 8.

Chapters 1–6 draw together what the 24 case studies had to say. Where they are quoted, their English (often a second or third language) has not normally been changed. Chapter 7 sets out five priorities and, in the light of them, ten '2015 Millennium Goals' for the churches. They are designed to complement the UN Development Goals not to copy them; though, like them, they represent a more urgent challenge than the date 2015 might suggest, which is why they are reproduced at the front of this book as A Call to Action. They include a proposal for a 'World Church Report on Poverty and Wealth' to be published every 3–5 years. The following pages have been written up as a 'prototype' to illustrate what such a World Church Report might be like and how it could be produced.

MICHAEL TAYLOR
Director, 'Project 21', June 2002

'2015 Millennium Goals' for the Churches
A Call to Action

1. Share liturgies and create new ones which engage with the realities of wealth and poverty and

2. Provide clear and accessible teaching and educational programmes on Christianity, poverty and wealth and on the economic order so that congregations are inspired and equipped to engage in structural change and bring about God's justice.

3. Define a 'greed line' to stand alongside the 'poverty line' in each country, translating Gospel teaching on wealth into concrete and contemporary guidance for Christians.

4. Organize a World Church Sunday on Poverty and Wealth in October to coincide with the UN International Day for the Eradication of Poverty to focus the attention of the churches on their calling to overcome greed and poverty.

5. Re-examine the reasons for supporting poverty-related projects and programmes to make sure they are advocates of fundamental structural change in favour of the poorest.

6. Give priority to local churches and communities in resourcing and decision-making.

7. Participate in national poverty reduction strategies in every country so that the churches make their full contribution to policy-making, implementation and monitoring.

8. Support and actively participate in an inclusive global alliance of the churches and their organizations (focused on the Ecumenical Advocacy Alliance) to 'globalize solidarity' and make church advocacy more effective.

9. Create an ecumenical network of research institutions to exchange and co-ordinate their findings on advocacy issues and make them available to the churches.

10. Produce a World Church Report on Poverty and Wealth in 2007 and 2015 to provide a framework within which the varied activities of the churches can gain greater coherence and reinforce each other.

The background to these Goals can be found on pages 69–79 and 84–6

1

POVERTY AND WEALTH

Poverty is still a major global reality. It has many dimensions – material, social and psychological – and many side-effects. It is characterized above all by a lack of income and power. Wealth is the reverse of poverty and is just as great a problem unless and until it is shared by everyone and grows rich in moral, social and spiritual values.

1 At the turn of the twenty-first century poverty is still a dominant feature of our world. 'Recognizing poverty as one of the most important realities confronting the world in the twenty-first century is beyond discussion' (*UN* p. 5). More than a billion people have to survive on less than a dollar a day. Some calculate that half the world is poor. In countries like Bangladesh, where 60 out of 120 million people are poor, poverty is the overwhelming reality. In India 320 million people are poor, a third of the population. In Ghana the proportion is much the same. In some countries it is higher. Both *Palestine** and *Colombia* speak of 60 per cent of their people below the poverty line. In the Philippines the figure climbs to 75 per cent.

2 With regard to poverty reduction the picture is uneven. Some progress has been made, in India and Ghana for example. In Bangladesh the proportion of the population in poverty has decreased though overall numbers have gone up. In Malaysia, a wealthier country, government figures are disputed but all agree that poverty has decreased:

> Official statistics suggest very impressive reduction of poverty in the 1970s and early 1980s, especially in Peninsular Malaysia. Although there are many reservations about the quality and nature of this data (part of the decline in poverty has been due to a lowering of the poverty line), there are few observers who would doubt that poverty has been significantly reduced. (*Malaysia* p. 28)

* Where the name of a country is used as the title of a case study it is printed in italics as here: *Palestine*; the titles used for the five themed studies are: *LABOUR*, *LITURGY*, *TNCs*, *UN* and *WORLD YWCA*.

South Korea reports an increase in absolute poverty in the late 1990s and *Germany* a dramatic rise in unemployment, and therefore poverty, in the same period. The major causes (South Korea's financial crisis of 1997 and German reunification), were temporary, though their effects linger on. In Nicaragua the situation has gone from bad to worse since the 1980s. The West Indies have seen a reversal of the modest gains of the past. In Hong Kong the situation is more serious than a decade ago. The Philippines face an accelerated rate of impoverishment and tend to despair of any improvement. *Russia* comments that 'poverty is everywhere' (p. 4).

3   Whatever the variations in the level of poverty, there is widespread agreement[1] that the gap between the rich and the poor, both within and between countries, is growing. *Hong Kong* refers to it as 'an unavoidable social trend'. In Namibia it can feel wide enough to speak of 'two Namibias'. *Palestine* describes it as 'a growing gulf'. *Chile* calls it 'sinister'. Others, like *South Korea*, speak of the 20:80 society or of rich people with anything from 11 to 40 times the resources of the poor. In Colombia the poorest 20 per cent receive 2 per cent of the country's income whilst the richest 20 per cent receive 66 per cent.

I think that in this country, there's a lot of difference between one and the other, because sometimes, when my husband's got a job, he takes me to Vitacura, or further uptown, I don't know what it's called ... it's another world, compared to the neighbourhood we live in. So, the difference is really great ... the rich get richer and the poor get poorer. (*Women's Group, Chile* p. 6)

Only *Malaysia*, whilst acknowledging that the gap is wide, believes it is diminishing.

4   Poverty is most simply described as a lack of the basic necessities of life. The picture is of men, women and children, the old and the young, without adequate food and water, clothing or shelter, uneducated and in bad health.

You ask me what poverty is. It is here, staring you right in the eye. Look at me! I live alone. I do not have enough food. I have no decent clothing and accommodation. I have no clean water to drink. Look at my swollen legs. I can't get to the dispensary, which is too far for me to walk. I have to walk a mile to catch a bus. I cannot see well. I can no longer do any farming. So don't ask me to tell you what poverty is. Just look and see for yourself. (*Grandmother, Fiji* p. 7)

It goes without saying that they do not have the means to obtain any of the things they lack. They are without land, or fishing grounds, employment, income, schools or healthcare services.

To peasants and fisherfolk, poverty means tilling the land of a landlord for the rest of your life and your family's. Poverty means having no land to till since the land is converted into golf courses, sub-divisions or plantations. Poverty means diminishing catch because mangroves are converted into fish and prawn farms; foreign large-scale fishing operations took over the fishing grounds. (*Philippines* p. 8)

Many of the more official-sounding definitions of poverty are couched in these basic terms. In Chile for example the poor have less than the equivalent of two breadbaskets per month. In Nicaragua they have less than the 'basic basket'. *West Indies* refers to the 'Indigence Line' which is the minimum intake of 2,400 calories a day. Thirteen per cent of the population are below it. In many countries the poverty line is a financial measure based on earnings. In Germany it is half the average national income.

5 While all the case studies speak about poverty in this basic way, most go on to insist that poverty is far more complex. It is 'many-faced', 'many-layered' and 'multi-dimensional' and cannot be reduced to talk of quantities of goods that are, or rather are not, available:

Poverty is a complex reality. People who suffer poverty live it as a reality which affects them psychologically, emotionally, spiritually, physically, at the same time it affects their family, community, and social relations. It is not possible, therefore, to consider any single dimension of poverty in isolation. That would drastically reduce our understanding of the phenomenon, as it would also drastically limit the possibilities and opportunities for action oriented towards its elimination. (*Chile* pp. 4f.)

Poverty has manifold expressions and indeed many roots. (1) It is about income deprivation. (2) It is about shortfalls in consumption and inadequate supply of nutrition. (3) It is about poor access to education and low physical asset bases. (4) It is about risks, uncertainties and vulnerabilities. (5) It is about personal security as much as it is about lack of food security. (6) It is about crisis coping with incapacities. (7) It is about self-development initiatives. (8) It is about dismal state of health and health care access. (9) It is static and dynamic, transient and chronic, sporadic and systemic. (10) It is seasonal as much as it is spatial. It is inter-generational. (11) It is about all known vicious circles, of low savings, low investment and low growth. (12) It is about the quality of growth and being left out of the growth. (13) It is also about personal freedom and alienation. (14) And importantly, about social justice. (15) It is expressed in each of these and all of these together. Given the multidimensionality, it is not difficult to see why all routes, income and non-income, should matter for combating poverty. (*Bangladesh* p. 15)

Besides the material aspect of poverty, two further aspects are frequently referred to: the social and the psychological.

6 *Social* poverty means exclusion from the mainstream of life. There are barriers excluding the poor not only from work and opportunities to make a living but from generally sharing in the life of society.

Back in their erstwhile villages, they [ed: the Dalits] were socially ostracized owing to the caste-factor, deprived of the right to be human and in the towns and cities, they are alienated and stereotyped into set occupations – the most menial and sub-human working conditions. (*India* p.18)

They have no social standing, no voice, no social ties with the better-off. They are isolated, alienated and marginalized from wider society, and do not see themselves as part of it. They form a social stratum of their own or a 'sub-culture' of poverty which is often regarded as backward. Worse still, many become 'discardable' as far as wider society is concerned. Half the case studies[2] talk about poverty in this social sense.

7 The *psychological* dimension of poverty is referred to by the majority of the case studies.[3] It has to do with the inner feelings of poor people and their states of mind. Apart from the obvious stress and anxiety associated with the constant battle to survive, there are many references to the low self-esteem of the poor, their loss of dignity, their humiliation, their feelings of inadequacy and even their sense of shame. Some come to doubt 'the inherent value of their humanity' (*South Africa* 5). Despite their own high standards, a sense of shame is fuelled by the squalor of their lives. They live in poor, makeshift housing often with dirt floors and muddy streets, without running water or sanitation.

We are going to die and we are not going to have decent housing, we are not going to enjoy the old age that is coming upon us. We don't have a decent bathroom, a kitchen. In the Summer, the stench and the flies devour us because we don't have a place to bathe, everyone with just a septic tank ... this is maddening. (*Women's Group, Chile* p. 5)

As a result the excluded can further exclude themselves. They are 'ashamed to be seen' or refuse to claim the meagre benefits to which in some countries they are entitled. Several speak of a pervading sense of hopelessness. Poverty is felt to be 'absolutely natural' (*LABOUR* p. 35). *Fiji* (p. 24) reports that 95.2 per cent of the respondents accepted that poverty, wealth and inequality were 'inevitable'. In Latin America

the old poverty used to offer the poor the perspective of social ascension, based upon small savings which were obtained after enduring privations or by means of providing children and grandchildren with access to education, whenever possible. The new poverty offers nobody such an alternative. It rather falls onto the poor as a fate of irremediable condemnation. (*LABOUR* pp. 12f.)

I live here today, me mother lived here before me and me children living here too, poverty is what we know for a long time. (*Agriculture worker, West Indies* p. 16)

8 In all these descriptions of poverty – material, social and psychological – one or two fundamental or defining characteristics stand out. One has to do with 'income'. If material poverty is not the whole story, the lack of a steady and adequate income removes the base on which so much else can be built:

Poverty is not only a physical state. It concerns the whole domain of existence. That means poverty is psychological as well as moral, spiritual, intellectual, ethical etc. . . . nevertheless, the economical dimension is considered as principal element to define poverty. Gainful employment can raise a woman's status considerably, but unless she is allowed to be employed and to have the necessary qualifications, the possibilities are limited. (*WORLD YWCA* p. 7)

Another fundamental characteristic is 'power' or rather the lack of it. Time and again the poor are described as 'powerless'.[4] They do not have the means to bring about change. They depend on others rather than deciding for themselves.

9 The picture of poverty can be drawn in another way by highlighting the various groups which are regarded as especially vulnerable. *Colombia, Ghana, India, Namibia, Nicaragua, Philippines* emphasize the rural areas and the plight of landless peasants and subsistence and displaced farmers. In South Korea most of the poor are in urban areas. *Germany* highlights the unemployed and in particular unemployed single-parent women. In Nicaragua and the West Indies the situation of children is particularly alarming. *Colombia* and *Palestine* refer especially to the elderly.

I'm Mathias and I belong to what is now being called 'the third age' category. Back in the old days, old folks were just that: old people; the old men of town. I've been living alone and abandoned for long years. My family disposed of me as if I were a useless piece of junk. I think that here in Bogotá there must be around 500,000 old people over 60. In Colombia? We are probably three million. I've heard that only 25 per cent of the old folks have any kind of social security, retirement pension, medical assistance, and aids like that. The rest of us depend on the good will of friends and neighbours to survive. Sometimes one of my grandsons shows up to give some money that allows me to half eat something. That's the way my days go by: in loneliness. *(Mathias, Colombia p. 23)*

The same concern about the elderly is reflected in comments from *South Korea* on 'fragile' groups:

> In South Korea the single household shows a high percentage of impoverishment. This is because many of the elderly who are living by themselves are poor and the percentage of elderly women who live by themselves and who are poor is the highest. This shows that the traditional social trend of one's offspring caring for their parents is growing weak, and that the social safety networks, such as elderly pension, public support funds or other policies have not been able to fill in the gaps. The fragile groups for impoverishment consist mostly of the elderly, women and those with little or no formal education. (*South Korea* p. 20)

Indigenous, ethnic or regional groups stand out in Nicaragua (Atlantic Coast and central regions), Ghana (in the north), Malaysia (Indians),

Namibia (San) and South Africa (Blacks). For *Ghana* and *Palestine* there is a link between deeper poverty and larger families whilst for *South Korea*, as we have seen, the reverse seems to be the case. This sectoral way of looking at poverty underlines the differences and particularities and warns against easy generalizations, except perhaps in one respect.

10 Many case studies[5] agree that women are the poorest of the poor or form the majority of the poor or are especially vulnerable. *Fiji* (p. 15) speaks of 'the feminization of poverty', about 70 per cent of the poor in that country being women. *WORLD YWCA* broadens the picture: 'Women and children make up the largest proportion of the world's poorest people' (p. 3).

> For poor woman it is much more difficult to survive and live than that for a poor man, as she cares about the children as well. (*Mother in Belarus, WORLD YWCA* p. 8)

Only two case studies (*South Africa* and *West Indies*) in any way suggest that poverty does not distinguish between women and men.

11 It is sometimes difficult to separate out the straightforward marks of poverty from some of its apparent and unwelcome side effects, just as it is often difficult to separate out the causes of poverty from its effects, as we shall see in chapter 2. Several case studies[6] note how poverty is accompanied by social disintegration including the weakening of solidarity and family life.

> I have been given notice at the age of 58. The way this happened made me painfully aware how much our society is characterized by social coldness and lack of solidarity. I have been working together trustingly for more than 30 years with those who have given me notice. This bond of trust has been destroyed from one day to the next. (*Klaus Bustorf, Germany* p. 9)

Violence, crime, drug trafficking and corruption are mentioned in many case studies.[7] Children are sold (*India*), forced into child-labour (*Palestine*), abandoned on the streets (*Ghana*) or, along with many women, forced into prostitution.[8]

> Susama (25), Hindu woman – came to Dhaka from Southwest Bangladesh with a relative who promised her a job. First child of a parent with nine children (6 girls and 3 boys) – father a marginalized farmer suddenly got paralysed and put the land on share cropping but

cheated and lost land. Suddenly whole family was under threat of
starvation. Then Susama headed for Dhaka city for a job and finally
placed to a famous brothel. She was interviewed on Bangladesh
National Television and apparently looked happy and asked if she
would return to a normal life if she offered with a secured job. She
answered in affirmative with a note that the monthly payment of that
job be Tk. 8,000 (160 dollar) since that much she earns or *must* earn to
send home to protect the entire family of her father of 8 and for her
own survival. A job of Tk.8000/month for a lady with no education is
simply *impossible* in Bangladesh and she never got a job (*Bangladesh* p. 4)

Disease and malnutrition become rife. The poor migrate from the
countryside to the cities and over borders into other countries.[9] The
environment is threatened and destroyed (*Bangladesh, Ghana, India*).

12 Originally Project 21 set out to discover how best the churches[10] might
respond to poverty in the early years of the new Millennium. Very early
on however the Steering Group, then the case study writers and above
all the New Delhi Colloquium turned the spotlight on wealth or 'excessive wealth' and 'greed'. They were seen to be as much, if not more, of a
problem and to require equally careful attention. The descriptions of
wealth are not as extensive as the descriptions of poverty, probably because for the most part the one is seen as the reverse of the other:[11] 'the
characteristics of the oppressed are exactly opposite to that of the op-
pressors. They are poor and weak and have no social security' (*Bangladesh* p. 22). The 'have-nots' simply become the 'haves' with money,
food, land and property, good health, education and an assured place
in society. They enjoy the comforts of life. They eat whatever they
want. Women's wealth often 'comes by connections to men'
(*WORLD YWCA* p. 3).

13 Two of the most prominent features of wealth correspond to the two
fundamental characteristics of poverty already referred to in section 8
above, namely money and power. First, excessive wealth is one dimen-
sional. It is mainly about money. Life is measured almost wholly in material terms. The wealthy are seen as greedy, selfish, hard-hearted and
lacking in values (though some of the poor are said to appreciate their
kindness: *Jamaica* p. 9). For many they are marked by spiritual poverty.[12]

The poorest the church, more solidarity one finds. The richest the
church, less solidarity is found. I am a preacher in a rich community,
but what I really have is a bunch of individuals. I don't have a community. (*Brazilian Methodist Minister, LABOUR* p. 48)

A different sort of poverty is thus endemic in a society guided by market values. First of all, even when affluence is obtained, it brings with it rising expectations for rewards. But simultaneously, rising expectations make rewards less satisfying.

More important may be the spiritual poverty, the poverty of the soul, the lack of creativity and imagination which may be an integral factor of material poverty, but which is certainly even more apparent in affluent societies. Although exposed to loads of information and opportunities, undernourished and overfed inhabitants of these affluent societies often submit to boredom – be it from genuine lack of purpose or other incentives for living. The result often leads to more consumption, endless need for entertainment and extreme sports or adventures to test one's own limits and get in touch with reality. Or much worse, to mindless violence, drug abuse or other ways of escaping or expressing depression, frustration, loneliness or lack of confidence in life and in the future.

Many of these phenomena are attributed to social alienation or to the absence of sense of community. While most people may to some extent consider the needs of the community in which they live, strong forces encourage the individual to care for oneself first and foremost. A Danish trade union recently adopted the slogan 'Be in solidarity with yourself!' as a way of persuading young people to join the union. Members of developed but secularized societies seem to be turning away not only from a higher power, but also from a commitment to each other and to society as a whole. (*UN* p. 14)

Second, the wealthy are characterized by 'the intensification of power'.[13] They are influential, 'maintaining the status quo to their advantage'. 'They have the ability to take comfortable decisions' (*Jamaica* p. 8).

14 'Interestingly, many people regard priests as rich, even though it is known that they do not earn high salaries. Maybe this has to do with the fact that priests have higher education and they normally reside in parsonages that tend to be better off than the average homes' (*South Africa* p. 7).

There is a wealth that is the result of capital accumulation, the result of a selfish treasuring of goods. Such is the north of the city, the north of the world. This follows a mentality according to which goods are out there to be kept in abundance under one's small hands, with no reference to the needs of others. One of the results is a life that is poorly lived as it enthrones wealth concentration as its only *reason d'être* and *summa bonum*. Such is not the wealth we look for. We do look for a wealth that should have the capacity to foster human bliss so that we may meet our basic needs and be able to grow as persons developing to its full our potentiality, relationships, etc. (*Fernando Torres, Colombia* p. 29)

15   Whilst wealth is mainly described negatively there are three ways in which it is cast in a more positive light. First, where it is shared by everyone and not enjoyed only by the few (*Nicaragua*). Second, where it is understood more holistically and is rich in moral, social and spiritual values (*Malaysia, Nicaragua*):

Excessive wealth is egoistic, greedy and only cares for itself. On the other hand, holistic wealth is one that views life, not only in terms of accumulation of money or possessions, but as a balance among the various components that make up life: education, health, home, community, environment and society at large. Hence, holistic wealth in contrast to excessive wealth seeks the essential and elementary and, in the process, does not deny it to others nor does it rob from the habitat its elements and bounties. (*Palestine* pp. 6f.)

Third, several case studies celebrate what are called 'the riches of the poor'.[14]

Please stop calling us poor. Our only poverty consists of our lack of legal entitlements to our land (rich rain forest). Without legal rights to this land we cannot defend it from invading timber companies and others (including landless farmers). Could you instead help us obtain these documents? (*Waiapi Indian, UN* p. 18)

The poor are not idealized. *South Africa*, for example, refers to 'a persistent attitude of complaining' and the 'expectation that someone else is responsible for one's misfortune' (p. 7). Nevertheless the poor are not without considerable strength. Though materially poor, they are not necessarily poor in spirit. *Chile* in particular speaks about their resilience, their solidarity with each other, their dignity, capacity for organizing and self-help and, in general, their enormous potential.

I was quite poor, rock-bottom, but the important thing about my mom was the faith in which she educated her children. She never made us feel like we were lacking anything. I started to work at age 15, and it was then that I began to realize how poor we were. The first thing I did with my work – with the sweat of my brow, as they say – was to save and save, for my family, and with that, I helped to educate my brothers and sisters, and I built a very pretty house in which I'm now living with my parents. (*Church member, Chile* p. 8)

16 And if women are the poorest of the poor they too are rich:

I have met many women who have taught me that abject poverty does not have to go hand in hand with the loss of dignity, joie de vivre, social relationships, hope and creative power. (*Germany* p. 36)

Poverty, today, is not totally manipulated. It has urged the poor to fight for their dignity. In these last two decades many organized movements have emerged. Could you imagine, 50 years ago, movements such as the 'Slum Residents', the 'Homeless', and the 'Landless'? A poor woman from my church who had no place to live, called me one day to tell me she was not going to the service because she was going to invade a building downtown. She was proud of what she was doing. Instead of going to the Presbyterian Church, she was going to fight for life. (*Presbyterian, LABOUR* p. 36)

2

CAUSES

*Poverty has many causes, some deeply rooted in history. Bad governance, 'natural'
disasters, personal qualities and cultural practices all contribute. The lack of
income and power which characterize poverty also perpetuate it. The global economy with its neo-liberal policies and unequal trading systems is regarded as most to
blame. The reasons why some people are poor and others rich are often the same.*

1 If the reality of poverty is complex so are its causes. *Germany* describes
them as 'many and varied'. *WORLD YWCA* produces a list of 25
(p. 9). *Colombia* mentions at least five 'components'.

The causes of poverty are extremely complex. If we were to analyse
them we would have to go all the way back to the arrival of the Spanish to today's Latin America. If so we would be in the position to not
only consider political, economic, social, and behavioural factors,
but also spiritual components. I would say in the first place that our
countries revolve around a well-established system that renders
them submissive. The conquistador gets the upper hand by means of
violence and coercion, and it is up to the one who is subdued to
obey and work for the interests of the conquistador. It must be
borne in mind that the social, economic and government structures
of the pre-Columbian cultures were wiped out. As a result, there is
a lack of sense of unity that impinges upon almost any attempt to
engage in the construction of the society, as it renders a failure the
development of a sense of belonging. Another devastating conse-
quence is the long-standing struggle over land ownership. As the
conquistador took possession of the land and snatched it away from
the hands of the aboriginal people, having secured the blessing of
the Church, new models were established whereby land ownership
is an entitlement that distinguishes the privileges of a few. The
Catholic Church has exercised the deepest and strongest influence.
Moral regulations, political attitudes and behaviour, social organization, and so forth are the direct results of the influence of the
Church, which established models of power that remain untouched,
historical changes notwithstanding. (*Jorge Munévar, lawyer and
university lecturer, Colombia* p. 5)

In what follows the causes referred to in the case studies have been grouped under seven headings: historical, economic, governance, land, natural, personal and cultural. Even then they are not exhausted.

2 But first, many note the way in which poverty is self-perpetuating. The characteristic marks of poverty become its causes. It is difficult to tell which is which. The result is a vicious cycle of cause and effect. *Chile* speaks of 'the reproduction of poverty' (p. 6). Unemployment and a lack of education, both identified by almost every case study as major causes of poverty, are the two most obvious examples of this cycle. Powerlessness and conflict, including organized crime, are two more.[1] Poor people *are* unemployed, uneducated, powerless and caught up in conflict; and they are poor *because* they are unemployed, uneducated, powerless and caught up in conflict:

> Today, in Latin America, as well as in other parts of the world, the excluded masses promote conflict. They have no alternative projects. Rebellions explode mainly among the youths, independently of their economic level. It is the violence fought through violence itself. (*LABOUR* p. 42)

Violence makes people poor and poor people are driven to violence. Vulnerable groups, especially women, find themselves in a similar trap. Poverty makes them vulnerable and their vulnerability contributes to their poverty. The traps seem hard to escape.

3 Several case studies[2] refer to colonial history in general and the exploitation and plundering of resources that went with it as a cause of poverty (though *WORLD YWCA* notes that 'the historical dimension of colonialism appears not to have been considered' by its respondents (p. 18). *Fiji* sees it as a watershed: 'there is no record of poverty in pre-colonial or early colonial times' (p. 9).

4 Histories vary however and many countries tell their own particular story. The West Indies now suffer the after-effects of a shift of focus in development aid away from themselves as relatively good performers on the UN Human Development Index. Since the end of the Cold War, attention has turned towards the East and towards sub-Saharan Africa, judged of all regions to be 'the poorest of the poor'. Uganda suffered under the brutal dictatorship of Idi Amin and from the civil war which followed. Fundamental upheavals in Russia rapidly replaced a paternalistic form of government with a market economy. *Jamaica* and *LABOUR* speak about the enduring legacy of slavery in social attitudes and relationships. South Korea made a rapid transition from

an agricultural to an industrial society and, in 1997, faced a foreign currency crisis with catastrophic effects. Nicaragua and the Sandinistas were at war with the US, whilst for many years Colombia has been in conflict with itself, the roots of the conflict being traced as far back as the arrival of the Spanish. Palestine's economy has been dependent on its often hostile neighbour Israel. In Fiji the attempted coup of 2000 was followed by a downward economic spiral.

All these histories, in their different ways, have led to poverty.

5 There is striking if unsurprising unanimity between virtually all the case studies, reinforced by the Colloquium in New Delhi, that the effects of the global economic system on the poor are largely negative. The exceptions are *Russia*, where it was not widely discussed, and *Germany* and *TNCs* which take a more measured view, though even here critical voices are raised: 'this global market system marginalizes increasingly more people – even in the industrial countries' (*Germany* p. 12). Many national economies were already in bad shape[3] but the effects of the global economy are generally believed to have made things worse. Wealth has not 'trickled down' but has remained stubbornly in the hands of the few. Meanwhile poverty has increased.

Excessive wealth is made possible by allowing a limited number of financiers and business mediators to reap the fruits of globalization while an increasing number of Palestinians become pauperized. Banks in the West Bank and Gaza are clearly not working as vehicles for development. The local banks encourage the population to save more and then lend their savings abroad. (*Palestine* p. 7)

Case study after case study expresses dismay.[4] *Ghana* believes that the neo-liberal economic policies of the World Bank and the IMF 'rendered over 88 per cent Ghanaians poor' (p. 10). *South Korea* concludes that globalization 'propelled by the theories of neo-liberalism' has now become 'a new ideology for many in the world. But contrary to its claim that it is making the world more prosperous, it is the primary cause and reason for poverty' (p. 36). *India*'s condemnation is probably the most vehement:

The poor have experienced globalization as a hurricane that destroys whatever comes in its way, leaving behind nothing but death and destruction. This is a challenge of faith. We categorically condemn therefore that globalization is demonic and dehumanizing. (*India* p. 24)

In a fantastically rich country such as Namibia that produces gold, dia-
monds, copper, uranium, and has one of the richest fish beds in the
world, babies are dying of kwashiorkor (a protein deficiency disease).
However, in the age of globalization, the fish caught in Namibia is
converted into pet food and fishmeal by the rich and industrialized
countries. The irony – big-bellied babies are dying so that the pets
may have 'low calorie' food. (*Namibia* p. 10)

6   'Globalization' or 'the global economy' usually refers to neo-liberal
economic policies including open borders, the liberalization of trade,
unfettered capital flows and free market systems. 'Everything has to
be brought under the fist of the market' (*Colombia* p. 12). One of the
direct links between this global economy and a particular country is
the imposition of Structural Adjustment Policies (SAPs) by the
World Bank and the IMF. These policies are reflected in the measures
taken by the South Korean government following the crisis of 1997:

> Thereafter, the South Korean government, in accordance with
> the guidelines of oversight presented by the IMF began to liberal-
> ize the markets to foreign investors, fully open the financial mar-
> kets, reduce taxes on imports, reduce the government budget,
> reduce and restructure many of the government's regulations in
> regards to economic activity, privatize public companies, restruc-
> ture the banks and other financial institutions, reduce the overall
> debts of companies, and open the labour market to allow more
> fluidity. (p. 37)

The reasons for these policies are to some extent understood. A government may have failed to manage its own economy and SAPs are intended to put that economy back on course. They are the conditions
on which any further financial support will be given. It is also acknowledged that in some cases, including South Korea, economic growth
followed the imposition or adoption of these polices. But in general
the effect on the poor is judged to be negative.[5] Jobs were lost, often
on a massive scale; wages went down; taxes, prices and the cost of services went up; expenditure on health and education was cut.

> As a result of the policies initiated in South Korea by the IMF,
> South Korean society has been struck with the sword of Structural
> Adjustment which has caused the weakening of regulation, the
> privatization of companies and the liberalization of markets,

rapidly increasing the number of poor who have lost jobs and who have no social welfare policy to care for their basic necessities. (p. 9)

India concludes that, as a result of SAPs, 'more people are trapped under the conditions of poverty, hunger and human rights abuses'. To make matters worse, 'poverty reduction programmes have been cut' (pp. 10f.).

7 Lending and borrowing money is an intrinsic feature of the global economic system, but whereas debts incurred by richer nations are sustainable, the debts of poorer countries are not and become yet another cause of poverty. They are an added reason for imposing SAPs and they lead to much the same results. *LABOUR* describes it as 'indebted de-industrialization' with low wages and high unemployment (pp. 9f.). What is spent on servicing debt cannot be spent on health and education services for the poor. 'How can you run a country on 24.7 per cent of the revenue collected, which is what is left over for Jamaica after debt repayment?' (*Jamaica* p. 24):

> The amount of money that Bangladesh pays in 1998 against debt servicing is equal to that of health and food budget together ... to support the health budget, Bangladesh in 1998, had to borrow another 556 million. (*Bangladesh* p. 20)

It seems like another example of the vicious circle. *Ghana* refers to the Heavily Indebted Poor Countries (HIPC) initiative designed to ease the burden of debt. It has still to prove itself successful.

The financial dependency of poor countries also has a preponderant role. The Brazilian foreign debt, for example, was already paid more than once, only with the interests. That debt strangles our development accentuating the difficulty of the population in having access to education, because there is less investments from the government in social areas. (*Father José Pietro, LABOUR* p. 39)

---

8 The trading system of the global economy is regarded as unjust and unequal.[6] *Uganda* complains that it has 'liberalized' its own economy while Western countries have not liberalized theirs. *West Indies* insists that the Caribbean should be protected from the full blast of international competition. It is highly critical of the dismantling of preferential trading arrangements for the banana industry in the Windward Isles. When trade is liberalized, the poorer countries are the losers. 'When WTO

comes we shall all be beggars' (*India* p. 11). Global 'trade' is as much in money as in goods, if not more. Liberalization is again the name of the game with the advantages going to the rich and not the poor:

> Not only has the globalization of the market allowed the free flow of speculative capital across the globe, but they are continuously seeking to reduce any form of regulation or legislation which might hinder their movements, thereby increasing the speculative character of their transactions. In such a context the extreme discrepancies in the distribution of the global wealth among countries, as well as the discrepancies and inequality of the distribution of wealth in any given country is drastically increasing. (*South Korea* p. 4)

The result is horrifying scenes along the borders of the rich world. Latin Americans desperately try to cross Mexico again and again to get into the United States. North Africans set out on the Mediterranean in shaky boats to get into Europe. Stowaways from all over the world are being discovered on board aeroplanes, ships and trucks. Migrants trust traffickers to get them to the Promised Land, often under inhuman conditions and sometimes facing death on the way. (*UN* p. 12)

---

9 Governments contribute to poverty when they are bad, corrupt, inept or weak. Three factors have contributed to the weakening of governments or the nation state. First is the overriding dictates of international financial institutions like the World Bank and the IMF and their Structural Adjustment Policies. Second is the power of the TNCs.[7] It is greater than the power of governments. They challenge the authority of the nation state, insisting on policies which are favourable to them and unfavourable to the poor.

Challenges from globalization

Even though these issues are not new, some aspects of globalization make them especially relevant at the transition to a new century. Power is increasingly handed over from states towards market. A small number of extremely large enterprises control economic resources larger than many governments. Furthermore, governments' will or ability to regulate and tax corporate activities is being reduced in many areas. Even though international trade is believed to have positive impacts on wealth on all parties involved, striking aspects of today's globalized trade supply sceptics with good arguments. With large corporations as agents, poor people use scarce land to produce food for Northern markets instead of supplying their own and local needs. Most of the profit from sale ends in the hands of the enterprise and Northern governments through taxes on labour and sale, while almost nothing is left to the producer and the producing country. Large amounts of cheap basic goods may be exported from a poor country, allowing for the import of expensive products for the benefit of only a small number of wealthy people.

One could say that Southern governments should take a more active role in ensuring that profit is left in their country. However, distribution of wealth through taxation of enterprises involved in export production is difficult due to international competition. Export production is very often granted zero or reduced tax in so-called Export Processing Zones. On the other hand, almost nothing hinders Northern governments to impose heavy taxes on the sale of exactly the same goods through VAT. (*TNCs* pp. 4f.)

India gives an extensive and critical account of the effects of TNC activities on tribals, Dalits and indigenous communities: 'the state in connivance with the multi-national companies have deprived the people of their fundamental right to life vis-à-vis their dependence on the "Jal, Jungle, Jamin" (Water, Forest and Land)' (p. 8). *Malaysia* calls TNCs 'super economic powers' (p. 17).

The third factor weakening the state is the market economy itself. That rather than governance becomes 'the mechanism of our society' (*Hong Kong* p. 4). It shifts power 'from the state towards markets' (*TNCs* p. 5). It encourages non-interventionist policies (*Colombia*) so that governments do not or cannot actively support development or promote the redistribution of wealth (*TNCs*) or adequately fund social services or pursue policies which 'complement the dysfunctional aspects of the market' (p. 16). *LABOUR* concludes that with the establishment of the neo-liberal model:

> The state becomes a minimum state, thus relinquishing its social responsibilities . . . the state's traditional role as mediator in both arbitration and guaranteeing essential services is being eliminated. The state waives the promotion of social security, thus fostering a 'civil orphanage'. (p. 11)

10 In some cases governments are seen as having the power to act but nevertheless failing to do so. They fail to provide the poor with what is often

referred to as the 'basic infrastructure' which governments alone can supply. 'Infrastructure' means health services and education; water, electricity and sanitation; roads especially in rural areas, and public transport.[8] Sometimes governments are accused of abdicating their responsibility to the private sector (*Colombia, India*): 'The state has ceased to be a guarantor of welfare measures for the poor' (*India* p. 11).

11   At worst, governments cause poverty because they are bad and corrupt.[9] They are bad because they divide and polarize the people instead of working for everybody's good. They destroy rather than nurture people's potential for development. They refuse to address social problems. They preside over undemocratic and non-participatory political systems. They are authoritarian. Their undemocratic character is reinforced by the weakening of trade unions and workers' organizations in the face of mass unemployment:

> Upon analysing the effects of neo-liberalism from the point of view of the labour movement, we see that the success of such policy meant a historical defeat of many of the victories and rights acquired by the labour movements during the long run. In several countries, like Brazil, unions are being forced to accept proposals from the government, and even presenting proposals that years ago would have been considered absurd. Now they come as the only alternatives to preserve work positions. (*LABOUR* p. 27)

The Brazilian labour unions are in a very deep crisis. They lost power in the nineties; the professional categories decreased in number, the industrial employment fell drastically. Today the unions have a secondary role in the national political scenery due to unemployment. We had a brutal fall in the number of strikes, in the number of days in strike and in the quality of claims, because these are 'reactive' strikes. They are meant not to achieve things but to prevent from losing what was already achieved. (*Renato Simões, LABOUR* p. 40)

---

12   Over half the case studies speak about corruption,[10] sometimes more politely referred to as the misuse or mismanagement of resources and public funds. 'Political tribalism' (*Jamaica*) or 'relationism' (*South Korea*) is one form of it, where family members and associates receive preferential treatment in the scramble for jobs. The extravagant lifestyle of government officials is another.

To the social deterioration that we have been describing, corruption must be added as an element that erodes the social fabric of the nation. Corruption is practically institutionalized. There are many scandals that daily come to the surface related to illicit purchases and sales of State properties, bribes, influences traffic, tax evasion, taking advantage of certain positions of power, ghost wages, use of public goods for political campaigns of the government party, embezzlements, etc. Such scandals tell a lot about the type of public officials that take part in the present government. The dominant classes bound to political power, have captured the positions of economic control, and their incomes have increased considerably in detriment of the standard of living of the popular sectors, that each day see limited their hopes of a better future for their families.

The problem is deepened by the governmental attitude, of not answering with seriousness in relation to the different cases in which ministers and other officials, as well as the President of the Republic have been implicated. The population points daily to these facts and asks how it is possible that while taxes are raised as well as water tariffs, electricity power and other services, government officers do not act with justice on these cases, and continued with unnecessary expenditure in the purchase of car pools, expenses in official delegations with personnel who have nothing to do with such diplomatic, economic negotiations. Among persons interviewed in our consultation process the opinion is held that there is a co-relation between corruption and national impoverishment. (*Nicaragua* p. 14)

Philippines describes corruption as 'the bane that deprives the needy'. (p. 9)

13 *Philippines* describes the monopoly of the land (and fishing grounds) by a few, whether long-standing landowners or large multi-national corporations to which the land has been sold, as 'the biggest contributor to overall poverty' (p. 3). It is a major problem in many countries.[11] *LABOUR* regards it as 'fundamental' (p. 37).

In rural areas represented by Hoima district, the cause of poverty was perceived to be lack of adequate farmland and high taxes. In one of the famous advice to the poor, the President of Uganda, argues that when it is raining the poor must tap – 'kulembeka' – enough water for their families. However, those who are lazy always tap little water that cannot meet the needs of their families and hence their poverty. In this example, the assumption is that the poor have containers to draw and store water. And yet from the responses of

the poor, their poverty is due to lack of resources to work with to
reduce their poverty. (*Uganda* p. 4)

14 Agricultural policies are also criticized. In some cases they are not
geared to increasing production and promoting sustainability; in
other cases they have not faced up to the need for change. *Philippines* re-
grets a structure which remains 'fundamentally backward, agrarian and
pre-industrial' (p. 3) whilst *West Indies* believes that an overdependence
on agriculture is to blame for adding to the difficulties of the poor
(p. 13).

15 Natural disasters make and keep people poor.[12] In some countries like
Bangladesh they occur almost every year. In Nicaragua disaster
struck in 1998.

> At the end of 1998 Nicaragua – as well as other countries of the Cen-
> tral American area – suffered the consequences of Hurricane Mitch:
> loss of thousands of human lives, several communities entirely disap-
> pearing – the most tragic case was that in the Leon, where a landslide
> from a volcano hill, buried entire communities killing more than
> two thousand victims – loss of harvests in the countrywide, damages
> in the ecosystem, in infrastructure (highways, bridges, breakthrough
> roads, etc.) and serious psycho-social effects within the population di-
> rectly affected. The days subsequent to the hurricane unveiled the
> crudeness Nicaraguan reality, as well as the weakness of a govern-
> ment unable to deliver in front of the emergency situation provoked
> by the disaster. Until today the affected sectors cry out for govern-
> mental assistance, assistance that only has been possible, in most
> cases, when channelled through humanitarian and non-governmental
> organizations. The effects in economic development terms are long-
> range, therefore the reconstruction process not only in affected
> zones, but also in all the country, deserves a national and international
> effort guided to give global answers in the different dimensions of the
> national life. (*Nicaragua* p. 15)

Although not regarded as quite so 'natural' as they once were, these disasters are surrounded by an atmosphere of fatalism which is only increased when they are seen as 'acts of God' or when poverty itself is
understood as inflicted by God as a curse or a punishment. It is God's
doing (*Bangladesh, Fiji, South Africa*). Some speak openly of fate and
chance and luck. For others poverty is 'natural' in a rather different
sense, passed on like a sad inheritance by the 'traditional poor' from
one generation to another, often sustained by religious beliefs[13]

which have kept the poor in their place and allowed caste systems, social discrimination and intolerance to go unchallenged.

Ever since I can remember, I've lived in poverty. My grandparents were poor, my parents and my brothers and sisters are poor, and I, my wife, and my children are poor, and we live in a poor sector. (*Group meeting with members of churches, Chile* pp. 9f.)

---

16 Not a few are prepared to say that poor people have only themselves to blame for their poverty. They are lazy.[14] They lack determination, drive and ambition. They suffer from low self-esteem and a negative frame of mind. They are unwilling or unable to help themselves. Blame is also put on the shoulders of the rich.[15] They are greedy and selfish and lacking in charity. The rich exploit the poor, though so do the poor themselves (*Jamaica*).

In the suburbs of São Paulo, poverty increases proportionally to the increase of the selfishness of the rich and powerful, of those who can increase their money and businesses, forgetting the existence of other people. Progress has increased, but that does not reduce poverty. The rich are richer every day, and the poor are poorer every day, because the rich ride on the back of the poor; the powerful take advantage of the poor humanity. There is no solution for the rich. (*Bishop José Maria, LABOUR* p. 38)

---

17 Several case studies point to cultural factors as contributors to poverty. Attitudes inherited from slavery persist (*LABOUR*). Gender inequalities make women overdependent on men not only for money but for new knowledge and skills (*Uganda*) and leave them without inheritance and property rights (*WORLD YWCA*). *Uganda* describes the failure of programmes designed to transfer or 'diffuse' technology and knowledge:

Such diffusionist programmes, as implemented in the modernization programmes of the 1950s and 1960s, failed because they did not take into account the social (for example gender) and class dimensions of the societies in Uganda. For example, men carried out extension work and yet could not reach women agriculturists because the husbands would not allow these extension officers to talk to them. So the new knowledge was passed on to the husbands who decided whether or not to pass it on to their wives.

Husbands always blocked new knowledge or technologies that challenged their power in their homes. This is how new technologies fail to take root. (p. 10)

More contemporary attitudes, associated with Western 'liberalism', are accused (*Chile, Malaysia, Russia*) of promoting individualism and a sense of freedom from social and moral constraints. They destroy the 'climate or culture of solidarity' which any effort to overcome poverty requires (*Chile* p. 14).

I think the question here is that we the workers have lost a lot of our values, we've lost the concept of solidarity, what social sensibility means regarding many things has escaped us ... I remember that many years ago, most likely if you asked your neighbour for a tea bag, he or she would give it to you. Not now, because now it's [seen as] ugly that I would go to my neighbour to ask for that ... and this is very rooted in consumerism. Last year I saw a sector of falling-down houses, with stones and such things on the roof [to keep it from blowing away], but there was the fierce antenna for the colour TV. So, those values have been destroyed. (*Union Leaders' Group, Chile* p. 14)

---

18 Overpopulation and large families are highlighted[16] especially by *Bangladesh*:

Bangladesh is already overpopulated by any standard. A country with 130 million people with an annual population increase of around 2 per cent has already threatened the future of the country and eaten up of all fruits of development achievement. Though the population growth trends in latter years have been slowed down, still this population size is a great fear. More than fifty per cent of this whole 130 million are below 12 years old leaving the impression that population growth was massive during last two decades. (p. 17)

Once again there is a vicious circle: 'while large family size seems to be a response to chronic poverty, it also furthers such poverty' (*Palestine* p. 13).

19 References are made to two other causes of poverty. One is that the poor cannot get credit from the banks (*Bangladesh, Uganda, West Indies*) and the other the failures of NGOs (non-governmental organizations) when they become remote from the grass roots and too commercialized and competitive (*Bangladesh, Palestine*).

20 The causes of wealth can be traced throughout this chapter. In many
    ways they are the causes of poverty working in reverse, just as wealth
    itself is the reverse image of poverty. Many factors, including the
    global economy, which work against the poor work in favour of the
    rich (*Colombia, Jamaica, South Korea*). Many of the things the poor lack,
    from resources to education and power, the rich enjoy.[17]

21 If poor people are seen as lazy, the rich are sometimes characterized as
    working hard.[18] In Fiji most people appear to think that is true (*Fiji*
    p. 23). If the poor have a negative attitude the rich are positive and en-
    terprising (*TNCs, Jamaica*). And if the poor are exploited, the rich ex-
    ploit.[19] *Ghana, Jamaica, Russia* and *Uganda* do not cast the rich in a
    good light at all. 'Most . . . believe that today, in Russia, there is not a
    single wealthy person whose riches are acquired honestly' (*Russia* p.
    15). Many, as we have seen, would say the same of wealthy countries.

3

THE TEACHING OF THE CHURCHES

The teaching of the churches is varied and confusing. It can be organized into four types: 'Spiritualizing' which tends to ignore social issues and accept poverty; 'Prosperity' which regards riches as rewards for faith; 'Liberation' which makes freedom from injustice the focus of the gospel; and 'Holistic' which looks for right relations all round between God, 'man' and creation. Wealth is seen as a mixed blessing. Greed is condemned.

1 The teaching of the churches about poverty and wealth and how they relate to the gospel and the church's mission is extremely varied, even contradictory.

There is no unanimity among Christians and their churches in their belief about the issues of wealth and poverty. It is even safe to say that there are as many beliefs on this issue as there are churches in our country. (*Philippines* p. 10)

Poverty itself for example can be something God engineers and of which God approves, or it can be something to which God is absolutely opposed (*Colombia, South Africa, UN*). It is not surprising that the churches' teaching is criticized for being unhelpful and confusing.

2 One source of confusion is the Bible itself. It 'sends confusing messages' which 'divide people's understanding' (*South Africa* pp. 8f.). Biblical texts can be heard in many different ways. Matthew 26.11, 'You have the poor among you always', can be heard to justify anything from indifference and resignation to sustained compassion (*Bangladesh, Chile, Ghana*). Church leaders and preachers are another source of confusion. They are accused of saying different things or not saying very much at all: 'the churches' teachings on poverty and wealth vary from church leader to church leader' (*West Indies* 19). *Hong Kong* found it hard 'to find a profound theological reflection on the issue of poverty from the leaders of the church' (p. 6); and while some congregations were grateful to their pastors for 'prophetic teaching' (*LITURGY* p. 7) others felt they received little if any teaching at all:

The Churches in Bangladesh officially do not have any systematic teaching and preaching on poverty and wealth. Neither do the theological institutions have any organized curriculum to teach their theology students and seminarians these areas. Sometimes programs for orientation and consultation are organized by different Christian organizations to make people aware about what the Bible has to say about poverty and wealth. But these efforts are of sporadic nature and not broad based and systematic. (*Bangladesh* p. 12)

Despite the overall topic being on poverty and wealth and therefore oppression and inequality, none of the five leaders interviewed spoke strongly on justice issues and the need for the Churches to be the conscience of society in a prophetic way. (*Fiji* p. 25)

All five of the leaders were disturbed by the prosperity preaching style of the new United States based churches – especially when they declared that people who were poor must be sinful. This was judged to be bad theology. (*Fiji* p. 26)

West Indies concludes that 'the social teaching of the church is the church's best kept secret' (p. 19).

Different social groups, rich and poor, are bound to have different perspectives on poverty and wealth (*Jamaica, LABOUR*) and so add to the confusion of voices. But their opinions are not entirely predictable. *LITURGY* found well-off congregations taking quite different attitudes to their wealth. Some were a good deal more uncomfortable with it than others. Finally churches like the evangelical church in Chile have changed their teaching in the light of their experiences so that new and old understandings live side by side (*Colombia, LABOUR*).

3 Whatever the reasons for the variety and confusion, the teaching of the churches needs to be clarified and improved:

It is clear that faith is central to understanding of poverty and wealth. A bad theology can disempower the poor, or distort the faith of the rich ... One of the crucial issues that clearly needs to be done to address the issue of poverty and wealth is the theology of poverty and wealth. (*South Africa* pp. 9f.)

Colombia and *LABOUR* find many who believe that the church's teaching will only be improved by taking a radically different approach to theology, starting with people at the grass roots and dealing with the realities they face in their daily lives. They call it 'Grass Roots' or 'daily' theology.

The meetings with these theologians evidenced that, in many cases, the institutional theological reflection becomes abstract and distanced from the daily problems. That is why the so-called 'Daily Theology' is necessary. It is based on daily concrete experiences, existence and problems. The 'Daily Theology' is dynamic, approaching new experiences and reflections through the people's situations. However, we noticed that many of those who are working with that kind of theological practice and with projects linked to poverty, have marginal position at the eyes of the official theology of the institutions. (*LABOUR* pp. 54f.)

---

4 The varied voices of the churches can be organized into four reasonably coherent groups or types: 'spiritualizing', 'prosperity', 'liberation' and 'holistic'; though neither these groups nor their opinions are entirely exclusive or discrete.

5 Some teaching makes a sharp distinction between 'material' and 'spiritual' and restricts the concerns of the church to spiritual and 'otherworldly' matters (*Bangladesh, Ghana*). Good news to the poor is news of spiritual salvation (*Philippines*). The church's mission is exclusively spiritual and it should concentrate on spiritual issues (*South Africa, Uganda*). It is about church growth through individual conversion, not social change (*South Korea*). Tackling poverty, especially its structural and political dimensions, is definitely not a spiritual issue (*Chile, South Korea, LABOUR*).

While Christianity is very strong in form and substance in Fiji, the style of Christianity that the nineteenth century churches brought from Europe tended to be based on individual piety. Fiji became very religious in the sense that people built churches in every village, were regular church-goers, read their Bibles, prayed, listened to stirring sermons and sang hymns in beautiful harmony. Sunday observance was strict and people were generous in collecting for the Church. But it was a style of Christianity that tended to be removed from the problems and concerns of the world and society in which it existed. (*Fiji* p. 19)

Aloisio Saguta was doing research on the Churches and squatters. He asked one Assemblies of God pastor what his Church thought about the squatters' problems. The pastor replied: 'We are not concerned

about the problems of the squatters; we are only concerned about
the souls of the squatters.' Yet, when Saguta asked one of the squatters about the Church pastor he was told: 'We only see him when he
comes around to collect money for the Church.' (*Fiji* p. 24)

The most that can be said is that if social change is desirable it will only
come about as individuals accept the need for inner conversion and
spiritual salvation (*Philippines*).

6 Poverty tends to be seen by this group in a rather positive light. The
poor are blessed. Their poverty keeps them humble before God
(*South Africa*). It is a blessed state to be in with privileged status (*Bangladesh*). It provides opportunities for spiritual achievement and promises
heavenly rewards and riches to come (*Ghana, South Africa*).

A TV preacher on the TV said, seek the godly things. We are chosen
people. Do not run behind the worldly things. Obey your superiors
and masters in your work. Obedience is highly essential. You get
more trials and sufferings because you are chosen people. This life is
like fire, you need to go through fire. You will be purified. You have
to offer yourself as a pure person to God when he returns. (*India* p. 4)

Compassion and practical help for the poor, in contrast to social action
against poverty, are not however ruled out (*Chile, Ghana*).

7 Sometimes a much harsher note is sounded. Poverty is God's will
(*Chile, Philippines, LABOUR*). It is God's curse (*India*) or punishment
for sin and ingratitude (*West Indies*). Little can be done about it, or
indeed should be done. Attempts to overcome poverty are 'anti-
religious' and sinful in themselves (*Bangladesh, India, Nicaragua*). The
poor should accept their lot (*Bangladesh, India*).

8 The motives for this 'spiritualizing' approach to poverty are obviously
open to suspicion. It promotes a form of Christianity, full of 'comfortable hymn singing', which supports the status quo and carefully
avoids issues of justice and social change (*Fiji, Palestine*).

The poor know what the non-poor teaches them. So there is fatalism.
The desire to develop is known as sin. Therefore, the poor cease to
desire, and lose motivation to progress. (*Bangladesh* pp. 24f.)

Some poor church communities however, for example the Assemblies
of God and the Pentecostals in Brazil and Chile, use positive attitudes
to material poverty and to the poor as 'blessed' (not cursed) by God

to affirm the poor and give them dignity (*Chile, Namibia, LABOUR*). They may 'consider themselves rich'.

People feel happy and worthy because *theirs is the Kingdom of God.* Pentecostalism reinforces the idea that besides being *symbolically, culturally and materially* poor, people may consider themselves rich, because they speak languages, they prophesize and they are blessed. Because they trust God is with them and everything is part of God's purposes, there is hope for the future. (*LABOUR* p. 46)

---

9 Several case studies[1] draw attention to the Prosperity Gospel and its growing influence. According to this teaching, faith in God will bring rewards not only in the next life but in this one. Those who give their lives to Jesus will prosper now. God's grace, God's blessing and our hope in Christ are all seen in material terms. They mean money, employment, houses and cars. Poor people can escape from poverty by believing their way out of it. Rich people can feel entirely at ease with their riches since they are a sign that God is with them rewarding their faith and hard work.

In a certain way, because of the growth of the Prosperity Theology, people are going to the Neo-Pentecostal Churches to solve their problems here and now, like, health, job, unemployment, etc. (*Ms Esther Abib, Christian Congregation*)

Neo-Pentecostalism is changing the way poverty is perceived. The Prosperity Theology understands poverty as a spiritual phenomenon. To be poor is to be a slave of the devil, it is the devil's slavery, and it is a curse. To be free and blessed is to be rich. The media (radio and TV) are partly responsible for the popularization of such conceptions. Many Pentecostal Churches, like God is Love and Assembly of God, are being influenced and the speech on poverty is changing. In the poor churches they still say that it is a blessing to be poor, but in the churches in middle class neighborhoods the Prosperity Theology is stronger. Many churches already have the 'entrepreneurs' worship service', a thoughtless thing some time ago. (*Rev G. F. Alenca, Assembly of God, LABOUR* p. 47)

Some see the Prosperity Gospel as serving 'the interests of that style of extreme capitalism being promoted by the USA round the world' (*Fiji* p. 20). It is in favour of 'material' blessings but is opposed to 'material' concerns like politics and structural change in favour of justice (*South Korea* p. 29). In Fiji church leaders who have little to say about social issues are nevertheless disturbed by the Prosperity Gospel (*Fiji* p. 26).

10 The remaining two types of teaching have a great deal in common. Both take a negative attitude to material poverty and believe it is not acceptable either to God or the church (*Philippines, Russia*). Both take a similar attitude to injustice and the unjust systems which include a few and exclude the majority. A concern for justice is central to the Bible, the gospel and the churches' mission.[2] It is 'the fundamental characteristic of God' (*Hong Kong* p. 7) and 'constitutive' of the churches' life (*Germany* p. 4, *Jamaica* p. 15). The churches' task is to denounce all kinds of injustice (*LABOUR* p. 50). Poverty is a structural sin not the personal fault of an individual (*Nicaragua, Philippines, WORLD YWCA*). Structures have to be changed.

Christians are called not just to the hope of a better life in the world to come but to transform the present world here and now so that all human beings, equal in their human dignity, may have fullness of life according to God's will for them.[3]

We do not wait for God to destroy this world and create a New World, but we co-operate with God to transform this present world and make this new. (*Bangladesh* p. 26)

For a Christian whose orientation is the gospel the necessity of a fundamental change is obvious. Change is badly needed for economic, social and ecological reasons. Not questionable increase of wealth for a few people but improvement of the quality of life for as many people as possible is required. If the churches don't say so they act not truthfully. (*Dr Helmut Wand, Leipzig, Germany* p. 13)

We 'need to de-bunk' all theologies which glorify poverty and expect the poor to resign themselves to their wretched condition (*South Africa* p. 13).

The differences between the two remaining types of teaching are differences of emphasis and tone. The one is more single-minded; the other is more rounded.

11 The third type of teaching, bringing good news to the poor in the sense of liberating them from poverty and injustice, is not just an aspect but the sharply focused, defining characteristic of God, the mission of Jesus and the task of the churches.

Christian love of the neighbour is primarily directed to the poor, the weak and the disadvantaged. The option for the poor becomes a benchmark for action. The experience of liberation from bondage which testifies to God's preferential option for his poor, enslaved people was a recurrent theme in the ethics of the people of Israel and a central argument backing the demand for justice in dealings with the weakest members of society. The right of the poor is grounded in the memory of the rescue from slavery: 'You shall not deprive aliens and orphans of justice nor take a widow's cloak in pledge. Remember that you were slaves in Egypt and the Lord your God redeemed you from there; that is why I command you to do this' (Deuteronomy 24:17f.). The prophets particularly condemn the injustice, exploitation and oppression that poison the life of Israel's society and foretell God's judgement on the culprits (Amos 2.6f. etc.). Their concern is that the whole community of God's people be saved, not destroyed. Hence their key message, that life-enhancing dealings with the poor and the implementation of law and justice are signs of faithfulness to God's covenant.

Jesus Christ makes the decision on the final community of persons with God dependent on lived solidarity with the lowest of the low. 'You have my Father's blessing; come, enter and possess the kingdom that has been ready for you since the world was made. For when I was hungry, you gave me food; when thirsty, you gave me drink; when I was a stranger you took me into your home, when naked you clothed me; when I was ill you came to my help, when in prison you visited me ... I tell you this: anything you did for one of my brothers here, however humble, you did for me' (Matthew 25.34–6, 40). The reconciling encounter with the poor, in solidarity with them, becomes a place to encounter God.

The unity of love for God and our neighbour takes concrete form when the preferential option for the poor becomes a leitmotiv for social action. From the standpoint of a Christian ethic, all social, political and economic action and decision-making should be gauged by the extent to which it concerns, benefits and empowers the poor. The biblical option for the poor is aimed at overcoming exclusion and involving everyone in the life of society. It commits one to see things from the angle of people living in the shadow of affluence and who, having no lobby, cannot make themselves noticeable as a social group. (*Germany* pp. 15f.)

God shows a preferential option for the poor. The Bible is very clear about that. So were the Roman Catholic Bishops at Medellín in 1968.[4] Karl Barth is also quoted in support of this view.

Barth declares that 'from the belief in God's righteousness there follows logically a very definite political problem and task' (Barth

1957:386). Barth is highly specific on the nature and theological orientation of such a task as can be appreciated when he states that 'God
always takes His stand unconditionally and passionately on this side
and this side alone: against the lofty and on behalf of the lowly'
(Barth 1957:386) this, and here he would agree with Gutiérrez, is
the concrete political tendency of the biblical message. (*Namibia*
p. 16)

God identifies with the poor to such an extent that to be on their side is
to be on his, and to mock them is to mock God (*Bangladesh, Fiji,
WORLD YWCA*). They are the 'faces of God'. He is 'incarnated
among the neediest' and his voice can be heard speaking to us through
theirs (*Nicaragua*).

12 Jesus is not only born poor (*Jamaica*), the poor are the whole purpose of
Christ coming to earth. The Beatitudes begin with his blessing on them
(*Philippines*). He is open to their needs (*Fiji, South Korea*). His central
message was to promise them liberation and his mission was to empower them (*Bangladesh, Chile, Germany*). 'Jesus' entire ministry focused
on the poor' (*Bangladesh* p. 27).

13 If God is on the side of the poor then, as witnesses to God's Kingdom,
the 'churches have an unavoidable responsibility to side with the
poor' as well (*Hong Kong* p. 1). If Jesus brings the poor good news, so
must the church. It is the core of the church's apostolic goals: 'concern
for the poor and concern for justice should be central concerns of the
church in any age because they were central concerns for Jesus' (*Fiji*
p. 18). Two case studies suggest that liberation theology is on the
wane: 'the Vatican has long since moved to contain the liberation theology' (*UN* p. 20); and: 'Discussion showed that, in practice, the
Liberation Theology is declining and the Prosperity Theology is
growing' (*LABOUR* p. 55).

14 The fourth type of teaching would not quarrel with liberation theology but might see it as part of a more rounded whole. It stresses
a number of 'both-ands' the most important of which is both the
spiritual and the material. We are not left with two incompatibles: an
elephant and a whale!

Are we finally with an impasse between a Western-inspired theology,
which gives priority to spiritual poverty, and a Southern hemisphere-
inspired theology that concentrates on material poverty? According
to Steve Titus, a 'sharp and divisive debate is raging among Christians
about the relationship of evangelism to social justice. The Evangelical

Christians are notorious for withdrawing from socio-political issues and preaching a gospel of acquiescence in and acceptance of injustice. On the other hand, Christians of ecumenical persuasion have been deeply involved in socio-political issues and have often disregarded evangelism and spiritual issues' (Titus 1995:44). Are we left, in short, with an elephant and a whale? (*Namibia* p. 15)

The good news of the gospel is about liberation both spiritual and material.[5] The church is an institution for both spiritual and material transformation: 'churches should preach the Gospel and at the same time bring development to the community they serve ...' (*Malaysia* p. 18). Social concern and personal evangelism are not mutually exclusive (*Bangladesh*). Combating poverty and preaching good news are both components of mission (*Philippines*) and salvation is about the person, the system and creation (*Malaysia*). *Germany* understands the gospel of the forgiveness of personal sins not as a way of avoiding a commitment to justice but as offering the personal security we need for getting involved.

15 Several references are made to the importance of sharing, both through personal generosity and by working for fairer social structures (*Germany, India*). The feeding of the 5,000 demonstrates God's will that the haves should share with the have-nots (*Nicaragua*). Stories of the early church in Acts inspire ideals of 'community' and 'fraternity'. Rich and poor are brothers and sisters sharing what they have to meet the needs of all (*UN*). *Russia* talks about 'Social Christianity'. Christianity is essentially a social religion: 'this corporate emphasis has been particularly strong in the Eastern tradition and does still constitute the distinctive ethos of the Eastern Orthodox Church' (*Russia* p. 14). Several other traditions insist that the resources of the earth are meant for all. God has generously provided more than enough as long as we share his abundance.[6]

16 Sharing is closely related in some case studies to stewardship. Human beings are not made by God to dominate and exploit and so impoverish creation and humanity. They are to be stewards of God's creation.[7] The Bible begins and ends with stewardship.

The Bible begins with the theme of stewardship and also ends with the same (Genesis 1–28; Revelation 22.18–19). It is because of man's negligence about that stewardship and because of his pride and greed that all the problems in the whole human society occurs. Poverty has resulted from the alienation of man from the Creator, from

> the Fall. The Bible also begins in a garden where humans begin to be
> responsible and productive stewards of God's creation, which pro-
> vides for all needs of men. The Bible concludes with the theme of a
> city with the tree of life with the rich harvests and fruits. So the Bibli-
> cal vision is a vision of life, abundance of life. There is no place of pov-
> erty. (*Bangladesh* p. 27)

Bad stewards make people poor. Good stewardship has no room for
poverty:

> God created enough resources in the world for every person to
> have a meaningful life. It is poor stewardship of resources that is
> depriving some people of what they need in life. If all will realize
> that whatever they have, has been given in trust by God for the
> welfare of others and share freely, even the poorest will have
> what they need to make a living. (*Ghana* p. i)

17 The vision of Shalom is perhaps the most holistic of all. It includes the
    material and spiritual in its understanding of salvation and goes further
    (*Bangladesh*). An option for the poor now becomes part of an option for
    all life (*Chile*). Peace and justice go together; God is reconciled with
    humanity, and humanity with itself, and all creation.
18 At least three sets of voices can be heard in the case studies responding
    to questions about the teaching of the churches. First are the constitu-
    ency voices[8] which tell us about the wide variety of teaching described.
    Second are a number of expositors who outline biblical teaching
    (*Fiji, South Africa*) or a particular biblical theme such as Jubilee (*Hong
    Kong*) or the historical teaching of the churches (*Russia*) or the teaching
    of particular theologians like Karl Barth and Gustavo Gutiérrez
    (*Namibia*).

> In the Bible, poverty is the characteristic of the oppressed. The op-
> pressed are the poor because they have no social standing. The autho-
> rities pay no attention to them. Because they are poor, they are
> oppressed; and they are poor because they are oppressed. The lives
> of the poor stigmatized by a vicious circle of contradictions. Bible
> stories show us evidences of the vulnerability of women as a class of
> the poor. The Hebrew word for widow, 'almamnah', has its roots in
> the word 'alem' which means 'unable to speak'. Thus the widows
> are the silent ones. The word was especially used to refer to the
> widows as helpless women exposed to oppression and harsh treat-
> ment and poverty. Widows in the Bible frequently connote not only

marital but also economic status. These are the poor ones, the ones without financial or legal protection. Orphans and widows were listed among the poor and helpless because they had no one to defend them and no means of subsistence. In the Law, the Prophets and the Wisdom Literature, only God is their protector and legal defender. God will hear their cry (Exodus 22.23; cf. Deuteronomy 10.18 and Psalm 146.9) and God will punish those who oppress them (Exodus 22.24). (*WORLD YWCA* p. 11)

The book of Ruth was one of the most popular stories used to define gender based poverty. Naomi and Ruth the two women in the story have lost all their men protectors. They are poor refugees and they are widows. Poor women are like the widows. They have only themselves and God to depend on. The poor have no power or means to speak for themselves, and they are always at the mercy of others. But their lives change when they meet Boaz a rich man. It is amazing that Ruth ends up being a distant grandmother of Jesus. (*WORLD YWCA* p. 13)

Third are the voices of the case study writers themselves and those who worked with them. Although it is not always easy to tell, we often seem to hear these voices and they tend to express their own opinions. They join the chorus of those who find the teaching of the churches confusing and unsatisfactory; and they never agree with the 'Spiritualizing' and 'Prosperity' types of teaching.

19 Apart from the Prosperity Gospel which regards wealth as a blessing from God and a reward for faith, the teaching of the churches gives wealth no more than qualified approval. Rich and poor alike are generally warned against it. It is acceptable only on conditions. One is that wealthy people use their wealth responsibly or, again, as good stewards so that it benefits everyone and above all the poor.[9] 'It is God's will for persons to have enough to live. Some are especially endowed to help those who are less fortunate' (*Jamaica* p. 17). Dire warnings are issued to those who don't. The story of the rich man and Lazarus (Luke 16.19) is quoted more than once.[10] A second condition is that wealth should be earned by honest hard work (*Ghana*). A third is that the wealthy should have the right attitude. Wealth may not be evil in itself but it becomes evil once it is the be-all and end-all of life (*Ghana, Namibia, Russia*). We do not live by bread alone. There are other things in life; and there are spiritual, social and cultural riches besides material riches (*Fiji*). 'Mindless riches' are the problem (*Uganda* p. 8).

20 God does not hate the rich. There is even a gospel for the rich though it
    may not be the one they want to hear. In a milder form it calls on them
    to share their wealth with the poor and exercise social responsibility
    (*Hong Kong*). In a more demanding form it encourages the rich who
    look for salvation to give everything away:

> on the issue of wealth, the Gospel is very clear. In the words of
> Jesus Christ: 'Sell your possessions and give in charity. Provide
> for yourselves ... never-failing wealth in heaven ... For where
> your wealth is, there will your heart be also.' (*UN* p. 7)

Some believe we can all be liberated from our self-centredness and
greed (*UN* pp. 21f.) and that it is possible to change the situation if
people, especially rich people, are changed (*LABOUR* pp. 52f.).
Others are not so sure and admit that 'the lives of the poor cannot be
protected by goodwill alone' and that law as well as gospel is required
(*Hong Kong* p. 8).

21 Two things are categorically condemned. One is excessive wealth and
    greed (*Bangladesh, South Africa*). The other is the neo-liberal economic
    culture associated with globalization.[11] It is castigated in almost apoc-
    alyptic terms. Its 'spirituality' is one of consumerism and materialism.
    Its 'ecclesia' or assembly of God's people is the market. Its 'salvation'
    is affluence. Its 'God' is money. Its children, including poverty, corrup-
    tion, unemployment, violence, ignorance and debt are 'the forces of
    the devil' (*Nicaragua* p. 17). It should heed the biblical warnings against
    idolatry (*UN*). It is 'nothing but Mammon' (*India* pp. 3f.).

4

OVERCOMING POVERTY

Many suggestions are made about how poverty and its causes can be removed, not ne-cessarily by the churches. Education, jobs and healthcare are prominent among them. More fundamental though are, first, the need to support and strengthen poor people and civil society as the agents of change; second, the need for good governance and, third, the need for a reformed economic system which, like good governance, benefits everybody.

1 The primary purpose of 'Project 21', including the 24 case studies and this 'prototype' report, was not to draw up comprehensive proposals for overcoming world poverty but to look at the role of the churches. It is impossible however to ignore the wider picture, if only because it is the context within which the churches are called to play their part. That is why many of the case studies contain ideas about how poverty should be tackled generally (they have less to say about the cures for excessive wealth and greed). These ideas are not normally actions which the churches are expected to take though they may well be ac-tions the churches might be expected to approve of and, as we shall see in later chapters, actively advocate and support.

2 *Germany* for example gives an extended and comprehensive account of a 'basic consensus on a sustainable society' (see pp. 19–30) and recom-mends a number of ways forward. It reflects the views of the German churches but no one is suggesting it can be brought about by the churches alone. The same could be said of *India*'s fairly full account of what needs to be done on a national scale (see pp. 20–3) and of *Chile*'s long exposition of what it calls 'social capital' and the funda-mental importance of building it up (pp. 18–27). Although occasion-ally a highly pessimistic note is struck and people seem to despair of doing anything at all, all the case studies contain some material of this more general kind.

The notion of social capital is comprised of diverse elements. At the individual level, the notion of social capital relates to the person's degree of social integration, his or her network of social contacts, the quality of relations he or she establishes, and his or her expecta-tions of reciprocity and reliable behaviours. At the collective level, the notion of social capital relates to the degree of trust among the different actors in a society, the norms and practices of civic beha-viour, the degree of association which characterizes the society, the existence of values and attitudes which help to transcend conflictive relations, etc. As much at the collective level as at the individual level, social capital implies dispositions of trust, self-confidence, self-esteem, assertiveness, etc. (*Chile* p. 22)

The academicians in our discussion groups tell us, that there seems to be nothing in the experience of the Filipino people as a nation that would enable us to judge as to which responses would be most appro-priate because since colonial times the poor have always been with us and they are just increasing in numbers. Then the wealthy families since colonial times are the same ones we have today as we enter the new millennium, except that they are getting wealthier. A few names have been added to the list of the wealthy, but they were those elected or appointed to top positions in government and every-one knows that their salaries was not the source of their new-found wealth. But for the millions who are impoverished, there is nothing to go by way of positive practical experience of resolving the issue of wealth and poverty. (*Philippines* p. 12)

3 A good deal of this material is directly related to what has already been said about the causes of poverty in chapter 2, and quite rightly so. Whatever causes or perpetuates poverty simply needs to be removed or reversed. For *Colombia* and *Palestine* that means putting an end to conflict and its repercussions. For *Bangladesh* it means amongst other things tackling population growth. For the vast majority of countries it means concentrating on education, jobs and healthcare.

4 The importance of education is underlined by 17 case studies.[1] *Nicaragua* calls it the 'determining factor' (p. 23). For *Chile* it is the 'priority area':

In order to adapt to a changing world – to make possible innova-tion and local creativity, to respond to the challenges of an in-creasingly interactive and globalized world – the education and training of people becomes fundamental. (p. 3)

Measures to check child labour should be undertaken in the context of population assessment and providing the needed educational ser-vices to keep children off the labour market. Also the development of a social security policy, with a clear stipulation for minimum employment age, can help stem the labour market forces that lure children into jobs which are poorly paid and without benefits and which infringe on the basic human rights of the child. (*Palestine* p. 11)

5 Education is needed at all levels: at primary, secondary and pre-school levels for children; at higher level for young people and as a life-long process for adults. The curriculum ranges from basic literacy and numeracy to skills and information technology. *Hong Kong* mentions teaching people their rights. Many believe that education should have a strong vocational bias, preparing people for employment or re-employment where new skills are now needed.[2] Special attention needs to be given to women's education. It is theirs by right, quite apart from any social benefits that some say it will bring:

> Nehru, one of the founders of independent India, once said that by educating girls, a nation 'can revolution[ize] its economy and its society' . . . it has been long established that educated women tend to postpone marriage, have fewer children and contribute significantly to economic productivity. (*Namibia* p. 19)

Only one case study expresses caution as to what education, or indeed anything, can achieve:

> While 53.7 per cent thought that poverty could be eliminated in Fiji through education and other targeted strategies, a surprisingly 11.9 per cent thought that poverty could not be eliminated. Equally surprising was the fact that 95.2 per cent of the respondents accepted that poverty, wealth and inequality were inevitable. (*Fiji* p. 25)

6 The need for jobs and incomes is also heavily emphasized.[3] Once again *Chile* sees it as fundamental: 'work contributes the medium par excellence through which it is possible to overcome poverty' (p. 30). For many countries[4] the agricultural sector is particularly important. Agricultural production needs to be increased in a sustainable way and, with it, jobs.

Current economic development plans, implemented by a corrupt, outside-influenced government, entirely contradict the logic of a profitable, agro-ecological development plan that could increase national production and decrease the immense trade deficit, while providing thousands of landless citizens a livelihood. (*Nicaragua* p. 24)

Policies must be reformed, especially those which disadvantage women and prevent them from owning or inheriting land (*WORLD YWCA*).

Work deserves to be properly rewarded and should provide 'a reasonable level of income for all' (*Nicaragua* p. 21). Some favour a minimum wage; others prefer to talk about a fair or just wage.[5] Either way, life may be more than income but it will hardly begin to flourish without one.

If we want to succeed in the eradication of poverty then what is needed is to adopt a comprehensive view of poverty – one that recognizes that it is more than a shortage of income. The 1997 Human Development Report introduced the concept of human poverty which focuses on 'the denial of opportunities and choices most basic to human development' – to lead a long, healthy, creative life and to enjoy a decent standard of living, freedom, dignity, self-esteem and the respect of others. (*Namibia* p. 13)

7　Support for small businesses by way of loans and credit schemes and more straightforward banking facilities, especially again for women, is one way of creating jobs;[6] though some, like *Bangladesh*, out of long experience, express doubts about an over-concentration on credit alone (p. 7).

Our development expert tells us that all the approaches and models in combating poverty in Third World countries are palliatives, designed to ease mass poverty, but not really to solve it. He cited several examples, like co-operatives and micro-financing, and pointed out the basic weaknesses in such approaches. (*Philippines* p. 13)

Philippines regards credit schemes as little more than 'palliatives' (p. 13). Government action to create jobs might include public expenditure on environmental programmes and social services (*Hong Kong*) and encouraging labour-intensive industries (*Malaysia*); but far more importance is placed on attracting 'foreign investment on a massive scale' – 'macro-credit' rather than 'micro-credit'.[7] How that becomes possible for poorer countries raises wider questions about the global economy (see sections 13 onward, below).

8　Education and jobs are closely linked in any attempt to overcome poverty by the need to 'invest in people' (*Colombia* p. 43) – teach and train them – so that they are equipped to seize opportunities for employment if and when they come along.

9 Healthcare, which means hospitals, clinics and medicines, is high-lighted by many of the case studies alongside education and employment.[8] The poor also need decent, low-cost housing, good sanitation and clean drinking water.[9] The campaign against HIV/AIDS and support for the victims of AIDS must continue.[10]

10 But how can these great reversals in education, employment and healthcare be brought about? *Chile* and *Philippines* warn against superficial answers: 'palliatives' or 'aspirins' are no substitute for cures.

If you will permit me the comparison, I think that we have a sick person with a very serious infection and we are administering aspirin to lower the fever, but are losing sight of the illness itself. (*Pastor, Chile* p. 13)

UN discerns just such an avoidance tactic in what it sees as a shift of emphasis from the 1980s onwards affecting the work of the United Nations itself. The earlier focus on 'development' gave way to a much narrower focus on 'poverty reduction'. In the wider developmental framework,

> the reduction of poverty remained an issue among others. The developmental political philosophy and approach to international relations saw poverty as one of the evidences of under-development and as a problem that will be addressed by economic growth and by other measures such as democratic access to education, health and other public services. At that time, an explicit focus of international action on the elimination of poverty would have been seen as a plea for at best redistribution of income and at worst charity. It would have been seen as treating a symptom rather than the cause of the disease, at the expense of structural reforms and fair rules of the game in trade and other aspects of the relations between 'developed' and 'developing' countries. (*UN* p. 16)

If education, employment and healthcare are ever going to be available for everyone we have to go behind or beneath them and tackle the root causes of poverty. According to the case studies, that will require good governance, a reformed economy and, perhaps first and foremost, reassessing attitudes to poor people themselves.

11 Poor people are one of the keys to overcoming poverty. This is sometimes said in a rather critical way as if the poor themselves were enslaved to a 'handout mentality' that they should abandon for a greater

degree of 'self-reliance'. In other words they should be more prepared to help themselves (*Fiji, South Africa*). In actual fact however that is exactly what they are often forced to do since they can expect little from politicians (*Jamaica* p. 9). In many ways self-reliance is also what they would prefer: 'following our own unique way and relying on our own strengths' (President Putin, *Russia* p. 11). Without being romantic about the poor, who have their own internal differences like the rest (*WORLD YWCA* p. 15), the starting point is to recognize and respect the strengths and abilities, the vitality and resilience that they already have.[11] They want to help themselves. They are well able to help themselves. What they need is the chance to do so (*Bangladesh* p. 16) and to 'seize opportunities for escape' (*Namibia* p. 13):

> Poor women working through women's networks have shown they have the capacity to establish their priorities, mobilize resources and negotiate the terms of local development with external public and private interests. Therefore, a first priority should be to support this capacity. (*WORLD YWCA* p. 14)

12 One fundamental way of supporting poor people and giving them more of a chance is by involving them in decision-making at all kinds of levels, national and international, but especially at the local level and on matters which directly affect their own lives and communities.[12]

It is significant to note that the focus of the poor of this rural community was very much on the community itself and the resources needed for improvement in the living conditions of all. Their desire was for more community involvement in making the decisions that affected them and in adequate monitoring of community projects and funds. No mention was made of the world economic structure and the national debt as being responsible for the poverty they were experiencing. (*Jamaica* p. 10)

Germany calls this 'subsidiarity' (p. 17). Addressing poverty

> is a long process of transferring economic and political power from one incapable centre of governance to another [presumably more capable] where the people are the locus and focus, the planner and implementer of programmes. (*Philippines* p. 2)

13 Much the same point is made in two other ways. The first is by emphasizing the importance of strengthening 'civil society', including

people's organizations, NGOs and churches, so that it can bring its own forceful influence to bear on government policies.

> On the other hand, the project – and it must be recognized that in the past 10 years, very little has been achieved – is to strengthen the organizations of civil society, to develop the 'third sector' in such a way that there is not just the State as a counterweight to the large economic groups, but also that there is a society which comes into play, an organized civil society, which expresses the people in their multiple activities ... that this be a living society and that this society permit, influence, determine public policies in such a way that they generate a greater redistribution of income. (*Humberto Vega, Chile* p. 14)

Some call this 'community empowerment'.[13] It involves educating for citizenship so that people can make informed decisions and are prepared to take responsibility and 'own' what they have agreed to (*Russia*). A second way of making the point is by advocating genuinely participatory democracy or the politics of inclusion where everyone, including the poorest and including the women, becomes a stakeholder and has a say.[14]

14 However self-reliant poor people may be they still cannot deal with their poverty in their own way without outside help. The external powers and structures that constantly impede the poor and disadvantage them have to play a more positive part. Good governance is required.

> However, many people believe that they must do something, and that the sum of small actions and local projects, together with an educational work, will slowly achieve a more just society. However, it is the work of an ant facing strong and huge structures. It is pursuing a new mentality, and that demands time and faith; trusting that God, although not visible, makes himself visible when he sustains these people in their historical fights against oppression. (*Father Samuel, LABOUR* p. 52)

Chile refers to 'social interventions' and undoing 'external knots':

Together with the internal, or subjective, factors indicated above, overcoming poverty requires that both society and the State open adequate spaces. It is evident that, in many cases, the poor are subject to external causality beyond their control. Without untying the knots which keep segments of the population bound in poverty, poverty cannot be overcome. Passing appropriate legislation and establishing specific policies and procedures are necessary steps for undoing the external knots which block the will and resolve of poor sectors of the population to overcome their conditions of poverty. (p. 13)

15 A number of specific requirements of governments are mentioned such as better social services, better roads and improved access to rural areas, but there are two broader demands. First governments should foster a more co-ordinated approach to poverty issues. They should co-operate with NGOs, people's organizations, financial institutions and other development agencies (*Bangladesh, Germany, Hong Kong*). Above all they should plan and be strategic. Poverty Reduction Strategy Papers, which have become a condition for debt cancellation, are mentioned with approval by several of the case studies.[15] Some give them a different name such as 'comprehensive development plan' (*Colombia* p. 27) or 'National Struggle Programme against Poverty' (*Nicaragua* p. 20).

The second broad demand is that governments should act for the good of all their citizens: what *Philippines* refers to as 'the new patriotic politics, i.e. politics based on a political programme for the good of the majority' (p. 22). Government policies should not just benefit a few. Their projects, like dam building, should not heap all the social costs on the poorest (*India, Philippines*). Corruption and the misuse of limited resources by an elite should be eradicated.[16] Safety nets should be provided for the most vulnerable.[17]

Social security systems must be based on legislation and, when possible, strengthened and extended in order to protect from poverty and deprivation those who cannot find jobs, cannot work because of poor health, handicaps, old age, or the necessity to look after children or sick and old relatives, families that have lost their providers because of death or divorce, people who lost the means of supporting themselves to natural disasters, civil disorders, wars, or forced displacement. (*Russia* p. 17)

Everybody's basic rights should be protected;[18] indeed a human rights approach should be taken to poverty reduction and development in general where governments are required to ensure an adequate livelihood and a secure social existence for all, not out of benevolence, nor as a desirable but as yet unattainable goal, but as a right. Human rights are a matter of law and any state legal system must uphold them:

> The realization of the right to a decent and humane standard of living as a basic right of society precedes any other rights that may be stated in the laws and regulations of society. As such, it provides an ideological and Constitutional basis for government policy which places priority in the allocation of funds and budget for welfare programs. (*South Korea* p. 39)

Three main types of human rights have developed:

– individual freedoms guaranteeing protection against infringements by third parties or the state in the sphere of personal freedom: freedom of religion, conscience and opinion; the right to a fair trial; protection of the private sphere and of marriage and the family; freedom of occupation and movement;

– rights to political participation, opening possibilities of influencing public life: freedom of assembly and association, the right to vote and to be elected, freedom of the press;

– socio-economic and cultural rights justifying the claim to share in the opportunities of society and secure chances of human development: the right to education and participation in cultural life, the right to life and fair working conditions, the right to property, the right to social security and health care, to housing, recreation and leisure.

The guaranteeing of these three types of rights depends on differing conditions. It is a matter of controversy whether economic, social and cultural rights can, and should, be guaranteed by government programmes. In any case, states are obliged to act for the observance of these rights. (*Germany* p.19)

Human rights are equal rights and government measures should be aiming to create a more equal society (*LABOUR*). This could well mean a bias towards the poor in public policy and spending (*Namibia*). It will certainly mean greater equality for women:[19] equal rights, equal opportunities, equal participation in decision-making:

> As women who consider themselves poor spoke to us, their clarity on who they are and what they need and want to be were eye openers. But how do they get on the tables where decisions on their lives are made? (*WORLD YWCA* p. 4)

The existing religious laws that govern the lives of the women of different faiths, particularly the Muslims and Hindus, needs a serious review to make them pro-women. Many laws have seriously contradicted the basic human rights under the constitution of the country. Women in general, under the provisions of laws have been made subordinate to men in all respect thus denying them of their rights and human values and dignity. Unless the very basic values of women are established, the much-desired development of Bangladesh will be delayed. (*Bangladesh* p. 19)

16 Good governance then will be strategic and conducted in the interests of everyone. The case studies clearly believe that governments should also play their part in reforming the economy whether global or national. They should intervene. *Russia* is very much aware of a continuing ideological debate between advocates of the highly interventionist state-centred socialist model of the past and those who now favour the neo-liberal 'free' market model with little or no state interference.

The main difference between the answers given by Russian citizens and expert opinions was ideological. The sharp polarization of those opinions is striking. Some support economic liberalization and the abandoning of the socialist model in favor of market economy. They say, 'Whatever may be said about the state as the regulator of economy being a great benefit for Russia, the only way to make people rich is to stop interfering with their earning a living on their own. Without the liberalization of economy, Russian people will never become richer, no matter what.' Others think that it is exactly the abandoning the socialist model that is causing so much poverty in today's Russia. (*Russia* p. 16)

Others raised the possibility of a complete break with the global neo-liberal model given its perverse effects and the widespread judgement, reflected strongly in the case studies, that it offers no benefits to the poorest (*Colombia, LABOUR*). In general however the approach is to tackle the fundamental causes of poverty that starve poor people and their governments of resources by reforming the global economy rather than replacing it and by bringing the market under firmer social control. This is the view expounded at some length by *Germany* in reaffirming the 'social market economy' long adopted by its country.

Wealth, not just poverty, must become a theme of political debate. Redistribution is frequently the redistribution of scarcity nowadays, because the abundance on the other side is hardly touched. It is therefore not just a matter of broadening the base of capital formation and distribution. From the social ethical angle the well-to-do have an obligation to show solidarity, and property imposes duties towards society, to quote the Basic Law. The capacity to share resources and bear burdens in society is not only determined by current income but also by wealth. If assets are not used appropriately to finance such important responsibilities of the whole of the state these duties to society will be only partly discharged, if at all. In a situation in which special tasks – like financing German unity – have to be largely financed by public debt there should be more recourse to private assets. How that could be done in a fair and constitutional manner is something that requires examination. (*Germany* p. 27)

17 National governments are called upon to redistribute wealth by progressive taxation,[20] to divert expenditure on arms to poverty reduction[21] and to regulate their internal markets (*Germany*). International instruments of governance are called upon to cancel the debts of the poorest countries and to redesign Structural Adjustment Policies so that they no longer penalize the poor but lend their support to poverty reduction strategies instead of undermining them.[22] Trade regulators like the World Trade Organization (WTO) need to ensure fair prices and more equal access to markets. Richer countries cannot expect poorer countries to open up borders to outside trade if they are not prepared to open up their own (*Germany, Ghana*).

The issue of debt forgiveness must then be looked at on all levels. They claim that much of the debt has been repaid through interest rates and the stipulation to purchase resources in donor countries or from lending agencies. The majority of the money that is received as aid must also be paid out in consultancy fees. Thus international injustice thrives. 'The debt is crippling us. How can you run a country on 24.7 per cent of the revenue collected, which is what is left over for Jamaica after debt repayment?' one participant asked. (*Jamaica* p. 24)

18 One whole case study (*TNCs*) is devoted to a discussion about regulating the activities of transnational corporations. They are often a law unto themselves, free from all governance and subject only to market

forces; and even those forces they can do much to control because of their size and strength. The case study argues for Corporate Social Responsibility especially towards the poor and their communities. It could find expression, for example, in respect for human rights, by investing some of the profits of transnational corporations in the future of the poor, and by encouraging governments to distribute wealth more evenly amongst all those who work hard to produce it. Corporate Social Responsibility will require social audits. Responsibility and accountability go together. Self-imposed codes of practice are not enough.

19 Two further points are made about overcoming poverty in general: one about the environment and the other about solidarity. The transnational corporations, along with governments and other players in the global economy, are called upon to take good care of the environment: not to downgrade or pollute it but to use the earth's limited resources in sustainable ways.[23] The vicious cycle whereby poverty and greed impoverish the earth and a depleted and impoverished earth makes people poor has to be broken.

20 Several case studies recognize the importance of building or renewing a culture of solidarity, in contrast to a culture of individualism and competition, if poverty is to be overcome.

Structures are not enough without a soul or spirit whereby people stand together, take responsibility for each other in families and communities and learn to reconcile their own self-interests with the common good (*Chile, Germany, Jamaica*).

5

THE ACTIONS OF THE CHURCHES

The four most obvious areas of church action are: charitable, service-providing, developmental and advocacy. There are many programmes, beneficiaries and actors. Education and training are prominent. Advocacy work is weak in some cases but getting stronger in others. The churches are active in less obvious ways as members of civil society and through the laity. Worship when related to justice is one of the churches' most significant actions.

1   According to the case studies the response of the churches to poverty covers a wide range of activities. They could be categorized as charitable, service-providing, developmental and advocacy. Charitable activities[1] include: handouts of food, clothing and money (*Palestine* p. 31 refers to 'outdated charitable handouts'); visiting and pastoral care; provision of safety nets and, on a larger scale, disaster and emergency relief.

2   Service-providing activities[2] include: health services through clinics and hospitals; provision of adequate shelter for the homeless and badly housed; employment services advertising skills and jobs; spiritual and pastoral counselling; legal aid and advice.

3   Education and training feature prominently in developmental activities.[3] In several countries churches run schools.[4] Fees are kept lower than in government or private schools and scholarships are provided (*Ghana, Uganda, West Indies*). Besides the core curriculum some education is extremely basic, for example literacy (*LABOUR*); some is for the very young, for example pre-school classes (*Germany, South Korea*); and some broadens out to deal with moral and social issues such as gender and human rights (*Colombia, South Korea, West Indies*). Training is mainly about jobs and skills in the building trade, agriculture, book-keeping, information technology, marketing, healthcare, dress-making, cookery and language training.[5] 'Capacity building' is something of a catch-all phrase but leadership training is part of it along with training for citizenship and preparing people to participate fully in civil society and local government.[6]

The case studies refer to a whole host of developmental programmes:

rural (*Bangladesh, West Indies*)
agricultural (*Ghana, South Korea, West Indies*)
community based (*Bangladesh, Chile, South Korea, Uganda, West Indies*)
health and hygiene (*Colombia, Nicaragua, Palestine*)
income generation (*Germany, Ghana, South Korea, LABOUR*)
environmental sustainability (*Philippines, South Korea, West Indies*)
food for work schemes (*Nicaragua*)
credit unions, banks and loans (*Colombia, Nicaragua, LABOUR*)
co-operatives (*Philippines, South Korea*)

When workers from Pakistan returned to their country, they asked
the church for support in their economic activities back home. The
church in response to this request collected enough money to support them with ten sewing machines so that they could begin a
needlework training center and factory. The two parties have
agreed to review the progress of their joint venture and will decide
whether to continue in the future. (*South Korea* p. 28)

---

4 The long list[7] of beneficiaries of these charitable, service-providing and
developmental activities is a good illustration of how extensive they
are:

AIDS victims
children
displaced
drug abusers
easily forgotten
elderly
farmers
handicapped
homeless
indigenous
orphans
poor
prisoners
prostitutes
refugees
sick
unemployed

victims of human rights violations
women
young people

In some parts of the Volta and Greater Accra Regions of Ghana can be found a dehumanizing traditional practice known as *Trokosi* which means 'Slave wives of the gods'. The practice requires that young innocent virgin girls are sent into fetish shrines as reparation for misdeeds of their family members. These women and girls suffer all forms of abuses. The abuse includes sex, physical molestation and violence, and gender discrimination. CIN (Christian International Needs) Ghana is assisting to put an end to the 'Trokosi' system and provide vocational skills to the victims. (*Ghana* pp. 24f.)

---

5 Advocacy involves raising awareness of the bigger issues that affect the poor (*Germany*); speaking out, whether in support or critically, about what governments, financial institutions and policy makers are doing (*Germany, West Indies*); and applying popular pressure through demonstrations and campaigns like Jubilee 2000 (*UN*). Once again there is a considerable list of issues that have been addressed by the churches:

   public services like health and education (*South Korea*)
   jobs, wages and working conditions (*Philippines, South Korea*)
   women's issues (*Philippines*)
   conflict (*Colombia, Philippines*)
   human rights violations (*Colombia*)
   debt cancellation (*Germany, LABOUR*)
   corruption (*South Korea*)
   respect for the environment (*Germany*)
   World Bank policies (*UN*)

Some issues are specific to particular countries such as 'Plan Colombia' where the government has been criticized for proposing a military solution to the drugs trade rather than one that undermined it by promoting economic and social justice (*Colombia* p. 27).

6 Two church actions are regarded as detrimental rather than helpful to the poor. One is fundraising when the churches expect poor communities to support the church financially beyond their means (*Fiji, Ghana*). The other is the church's unholy alliance with capitalism. Through returns on its investments the church profits from a system that harms and excludes the poorest (*India*).

7 Having looked at the main activities (charitable, service-providing,

developmental and advocacy), who are the main actors? The word 'church' turns out to be more varied than it looks. It refers of course to the local churches (*Fiji, Namibia*) which *Chile* calls 'primary groups', and to the churches and their boards and synods at district, regional and national levels. In Russia for example each diocese (the Russian Orthodox Church has 128) has a department in charge of charitable action and social work and a Department of Social Service and Charity at the level of the Holy Synod (*Russia* p. 19). Diakonisches Werk looks like its counterpart in the German churches. There are also various 'orders' in the churches, such as the Sisters of St Joseph and the Sisters of Rosary mentioned by *South Korea*.

8 After that come what might be described as the 'agencies' or relief and development organizations of the churches which act in response to poverty in their name and on their behalf. Many are mentioned as participating in the case studies (*India* pp. 27f., for example) and as sources of funding. Some are denominational like the Catholic charity St Vincent de Paul Society (*Fiji, Jamaica, Palestine*) and relief and development agencies like the Adventist Development Relief Agency, Bread for the World and other so-called 'Northern agencies',[8] Catholic relief services, Caritas and the Lutheran World Federation (*Bangladesh, Ghana, LABOUR*). Others are ecumenical. *Bangladesh* mentions CCDB (Churches Commission for Development in Bangladesh) and the Christian Healthcare Programme; *South Korea* mentions industrial mission and South Korean Christian Co-operation for Social Development; *Colombia* mentions the National Ecumenical Women's network; and there are several references to national councils of churches like that in the Middle East (*Palestine, South Korea*).

9 There are at least three more 'actors'. First are the church-owned institutions, mainly schools and hospitals.[9] Second are 'Christian organizations working for social justice' (*Hong Kong* p. 6) which the churches support but do not own. The World YWCA, if it feels close enough to the churches, might be an example. GRENCODA (Grenada Community Development Agency), whose work is very fully described in *West Indies*, is certainly one: 'the Church is represented in an unofficial capacity in this agency – Board/Staff profess the Christian faith' (*West Indies* p. 4).

GRENCODA operates on an annual budget of approximately EC$600,000 (US$225,000) about 5 per cent of which are raised locally. The major external funding sources to date have been church-based agencies in Europe and North America such as Bread for the World,

CAFOD, United Church of Canada, United Methodist Church and
United Nations Agencies – UNICEF and UNIFEM. (*West Indies* p. 6)

Third, *Fiji* and *West Indies* refer to inter-faith groups at local and
national level where the churches work on poverty related issues with
other religious communities.

10 Because the case studies are mainly country-based, the contribution of
important international actors like the WCC receives scarcely any attention (*UN*).

11 The general impression given by the case studies as a whole is that there
is a very considerable amount of church activity in response to poverty,
direct and less direct, through agencies and other organizations, and
that it ranges widely from charity work to advocacy. Some churches
however are criticized for their lack of involvement. A Malaysian
civil servant comments that 'at the local church I am afraid to say not
much has been done' (*Malaysia* p. 18). Again: 'Generally speaking the
churches in Hong Kong do not take the issue of poverty seriously'
(*Hong Kong* p. 6).

In South Korea, with the exception of the Minjung, the churches,
especially prior to the economic crisis of 1997, 'were intent only on
the growth of their constituency and focused primarily on the activities
of their individual churches' (*South Korea* p. 49).

– The South Korean church is quite weak in providing a programma-
tic and strategic effort to support the economically marginalized
and to eradicate poverty. As was already alluded to in the document, most South Korean churches are more concerned with individual church growth and remain weak in social interest.

– For example, the little resources which are set aside by the churches
for social programs are concentrated only on those in need who are
members of that given church. The scholarships that the church
provides for students in school are also mostly given to students
who are members of the church, and that only to those who are in
the top 10 per cent of their class. This is a direct negative reflection
of the competitive character of society in the life of the church.

– Many in the South Korean churches still regard churches and individuals involved in social justice issues as being radical and liberal
in theology.

– Although there are differences among churches and according to
the pastoral emphasis of the pastor, the South Korean church still
significantly lacks a strategic program for eradicating poverty.

> – The churches seemed to take an interest in social issues during the
> first phase of the economic crisis, but today that interest has dra-
> matically faded out. The decrease in offerings to the churches due
> to decrease in personal income has caused the churches to reduce
> their expenditures, and most funds have been focused on the main-
> tenance of church facilities and existing ministry programs. (*South
> Korea* p. ii)

Some churches, whilst involved in charitable, service provision and
developmental work, put less emphasis on advocacy. The churches in
Fiji are criticized for failing to be prophetic and for being more concerned about charity than justice (*Fiji* pp. 21f.). In Palestine:

> Up till now the Church has not provided a systemic input into the
> societal deliberations, whether formal or informal, on matters of
> poverty and social policy. (*Palestine* p. 30)

In Chile and Colombia the advocacy work of the churches is thought to
be getting stronger. In Chile Evangelical churches and leaders have
become more involved over the last ten years (*Chile* p. 27). In Colombia
the churches have long worked alongside the less fortunate but:

> What is new in both Catholic and Evangelical settings is the emer-
> gence of organisms and institutions that speak up against the con-
> stant violation of human rights, and make their best to champion
> the cause of the victims. (*Colombia* p. 35)

12 To end this account of the actions of the churches at this point however
would be to ignore two 'hidden' areas of activity that could be as significant as all the rest. One is where the churches act as part of civil society,
engaging and co-operating with governments and the private sector
alongside other voluntary agencies, people's organizations, trade
unions and NGOs (*Jamaica, Namibia*). *Nicaragua* explicitly lists the
efforts of the churches 'either as their own or accomplished along
with other organizations of the community' (p. 19). *Chile* describes
the churches as 'part of civil society' (p. 27). In South Korea by the
mid-1990s much of the work that the Minjung churches had been
solely undertaking 'began to be the responsibility of the local government and the civil organizations' (*South Korea* p. 26).

13 The second 'hidden' area is where the churches are active by virtue of
the fact that their members are present as Christians in almost every

place. Sometimes they form their own groups that may remain close to the churches or, where the churches themselves refuse to act, grow distant from them (*Germany, Palestine, LABOUR*). *LABOUR* confesses to some difficulty in discovering what exactly the churches do do, partly because of incomplete records but partly because of what was being done by these independent Christian groups:

> we discovered a very interesting fact, that the great part of the existent projects, they are developed by people or groups linked to churches and not for the ecclesiastical institutions (for the churches itself). A lot of times a project accomplished by a group of a church, for instance Presbyterian Church, is confused as being an institutional project, when in reality the project belongs to a group that frequents the church. It is very frequent in the Pentecostal churches and also in the spiritualistic orientation groups. (*LABOUR* p. 60)

More often than not, however, Christians don't form groups but are simply 'there' as individual workers and participants in government, industry and commerce, social services and the organizations and networks of civil society. The case studies on the United Nations, transnational corporations and the labour movement (*UN, TNCs, LABOUR*) are reminders of just how much 'church' activity is in fact the activity of church members: the laity. It is not discrete and it does not necessarily stand out from the activity of many other people (*Ghana, Jamaica, Palestine*). It is not labelled 'church' and does not seek to be.

14 Finally worship or liturgy is the most regular and frequent action of the churches. It can be divorced from issues of poverty and wealth and often is, either because the worshippers, rich and poor, prefer to escape for a while and not think about them (*Ghana, LITURGY*) or because such matters are not thought to be the primary business of worship even if they are the business of the church:

> The desire to express faith in a reasoned way, and the concern to live a Godly life may be by-products of worship but neither of these things constitute the primary purpose of worship. The essence of worship is 'to praise and enjoy God'. (*LITURGY* p. 3)

Where the churches 'hold in creative tension aesthetics and ethics' (*LITURGY* p. 4) and worship is related to poverty and wealth, in its hymns and songs, intercessions, preaching and teaching, offertory, announcements and the understanding of the Eucharist, then it becomes a highly significant action of the churches and in three respects. First, it can sustain the members of the congregation in the midst of their own 'continuing hurt and brokenness' (*LITURGY* p. 10). It provides support and strength. When discussing the place of indigenous music and song in worship, *LITURGY* comments that 'a community which is culturally strong and vibrant is better able to face and overcome poverty' (p. iii). Second, it can foster a sense of world-wide solidarity especially as bread is broken and shared (*LITURGY* p. 15).

> People expect from worship to experience a sense of solidarity in suffering and in celebration. They come to worship because they enjoy being together. The relationships are meaningful to them, they find support and strength when they need it, and they find the challenge to be there for others in the community. This is how they most consciously connect with issues and concerns arising out of poverty and wealth. (*LITURGY* p. 16)

Third, it becomes a never-ending process of spiritual formation and transformation (*South Korea* p. 25).

> Much of my attitude to life and how we should behave towards others and to social issues has been shaped by my years at this church and by a line of ministers who have preached in the prophetic tradition. (*LITURGY* p. 7)

Germany regards working for 'a value orientation securing the good of all' as central to the churches' competence and mandate and one of 'the most significant church options for action'. This orientation is to be inculcated in the general population, not just church-goers, and by various means including education and what is referred to as proclamation to individuals and structures (pp. 4, 32f.).

> The proclamation of the Word of God, his love of all people, is at the centre of church action. The church witnesses to God's love and his claim to the whole of life. A life by God's grace removes the fear of losing out and gives courage and confidence for action. This proclamation is not just directed towards individuals with their inalienable freedom, but also towards the structural – social, cultural and economic – conditions of their existence. The churches must not settle more or less comfortably into a niche in the pluralist society. Their

proclamation has to prove itself as they become leaven for a social order founded on justice and solidarity. (*Germany* p. 32)

But liturgy can certainly function in this way. In verbal and non-verbal ways, through sights and sounds (*Jamaica* p. 28), actions and attitudes the church communicates its teaching and allows faith to shape and sustain commitment to the poor; and that is what some Christian social activists have come to demand and expect (*Nicaragua* p. 20).

6

RECOMMENDATIONS

The churches are recommended to co-operate more closely and realize their potential to be a powerful global alliance against poverty. Advocacy is stressed but not to the exclusion of projects and programmes. Relationships need to be more equal. More adequate Christian teaching is stressed and the need for churches to practise what they teach. Local congregations are places where ideals can be realized in life and worship.

1 When it comes to recommendations, a good deal has already been said about what the churches should do in response to poverty and wealth in the early years of the twenty-first century, in chapters 4 and 5 of this report on 'Overcoming Poverty' in general and 'The Actions of the Churches', especially where the churches are identified with civil society. Some case studies make their recommendations almost entirely in those terms. They address NGOs and voluntary organizations, of which the churches are examples, rather than the churches as such. What is expected of civil society is by implication expected of the churches.[1] There is no real suggestion in all of this that civil society and the churches should stop what they are doing about poverty and start doing something else. The recommendations that follow tend to build on those more general proposals and the existing actions of the churches and seem to be regarded by the case study writers as consistent with what has gone before.

2 Some recommendations are highly specific to regional bodies like CLAI (Latin American Council of Churches) or CCA (Christian Conference of Asia) and to churches in particular countries. *India* for example calls on the Indian churches to end their alliance with global capitalism and their marginalization of Dalits. *Colombia* wants churches in the North to protest at the imposition of a neo-liberal agenda on Colombia, and its own churches to get together ecumenically and join in the national peace process. *Ghana* would like to see local church development offices set up, while *Bangladesh* looks for younger church leaders and more dialogue between the churches and people of other faiths. Both *Bangladesh* and *LABOUR* call for the better use of church

buildings in their countries for social purposes, and several case studies are especially concerned that their churches should speak out against corruption in government circles (*Colombia, Ghana, Uganda*). *Philippines* wants the churches to help safeguard access to forests and fishing grounds – what it calls 'commons' (p. 17), whilst *Jamaica* asks them to persuade the state to accept music making as a major sector of Jamaica's formal economy. *Palestine* presents children and young people as 'the most crucial demographic component of the Palestinian population' and looks to the churches and other non-government partners to work for a Palestinian national plan of action.

At this stage of the impending declaration of the Palestinian State, the Church in Palestine needs to have a clear input and contribution. It needs to play a part in shaping the future of the Palestinian State to the advantage of all its citizens and towards an accountable, responsible and responsive society. It is not enough for the Church to see itself as the guardian of the Holy Places and to minimize accordingly the role it is expected to play in ensuring a fair and just society. By combining the two functions, the Church will truly fulfil its vocation and will promote the kind of society that will best preserve and guard the holy places in an environment characterized by openness and religious pluralism. (*Palestine* p. 30)

More information about these highly contextual recommendations can be found in the relevant case studies themselves.

3 Loyal to the brief they all agreed to follow, the case study writers made recommendations to the churches at the global, national and local levels, and to their organizations and agencies. As it happens however, a number of these recommendations cut across those categories and apply to all levels, especially the national and international. They can be grouped under five headings: co-operation, advocacy, relationships, teaching and integrity.

4 First comes a strong vote for co-operation between the churches and, wider still, between the churches, other NGOs and even government departments in a joint, collective effort to overcome poverty.[2] Whereas some complain of a lack of co-ordination and even rivalry, all the players must now act together. The language varies but the point is much the same. Some talk of 'networks' from local to global (*Chile, LABOUR, UN*), others of 'round tables' (*Germany, Palestine*), and others of 'alliances' (*Ghana, Russia*). On the international scale there are grandiose references to 'the globalization of solidarity' and 'a

counter-hegemonic block'.[3] In all of these what matters is that churches and organizations come together in a unified way with a common, united vision, a united approach, such as a nationally agreed poverty reduction strategy for example (*Philippines* p. 17) with everyone moving in the same direction and taking a clear and united stand.

We must develop a unified view and perspective of the current trend of economic globalization and global co-operation. The World-wide Ecumenical Family needs to offer a unified action to the problem of poverty. It can no longer be seen as a problem of the poor alone. It is important that we do not allow geo-regional perspectives, that of belonging to the wealthy North and the other being the poor South, divide our sense of responsibility and actions. There needs to be a new ecumenical sense of identity, which allows the World-wide Church to join and unite in action. Our common witness and faith must result in united action to the problem of poverty. (*South Africa* p. 11)

The language of unity is quite strong.

5 There are those who seriously question whether such a high degree of unity is possible. Thoroughgoing co-operation where 'the state, the corporate community, the Labour unions, non-governmental organizations and the church are playing on the same team' (*Bishop Gunmar Stalsett, TNCs,* chapter II, p. 23) may be little more than a Utopian dream.

Is it really possible to expect to unite with the wealthy and people in authority on a common framework in viewing the realities of the poor and marginalized? Whose interests will they ultimately protect?

The wealthy and people in authority have almost always managed to get the poor and marginalized to unite with them in viewing the realities of the latter. By making use of the various cultural apparatus in society, the views of the rich and powerful become the dominant ideology that dominate the consciousness of a given society, including those of the poor. That is how they managed to hold on to their wealth and power.

Sometimes, even those who sincerely believe that they are working for the poor and the marginalized, wittingly or unwittingly make use of the framework of the rich and powerful so the victims end up being misled by these well-meaning people.

In the end, it is really impossible to have a common framework between the oppressed and the oppressor, between the exploited and

> the exploiter. The poor and the marginalized must come up with their own framework so they can liberate themselves from poverty and injustice. (*Philippines* p. 18)

Even among the churches, with their own deep divisions between rich and poor, powerful church institutions and marginalized church members, it may be too much to hope for.[4] Nevertheless a global network of churches is potentially one of the largest NGOs in the world and, if well co-ordinated, could become a very powerful force to reckon with: 'the ecumenical community has the possibility of converting numerous poor people's struggles against different enterprises into a global struggle' (*TNCs* p. 9).

> The churches are the world's largest non-governmental organizations in terms of members, and in many spheres the most influential. Christians all over the world are both political constituents and consumers. Some Christian individuals and many Churches are also indirect shareholders of corporations, making them a direct part in the enormous exchange of economic resources between rich and poor, North and South. In addition to the Churches' special role in issues of values, all these factors serve to make the ecumenical community a vital part in mobilizing and advocating for changes in structures and policies to make enterprises agents and tools for narrowing the gap between wealthy and poor. (*TNCs* p. 11)

6 A second group of recommendations comes under the heading of advocacy. Like co-operation, it is heavily underlined.[5] Again different words are used for it including 'being prophetic' (*India, Jamaica*), 'lobbying' (*India*), engaging in 'emancipatory politics' (*Uganda*), 'campaigning' (*Philippines*), speaking out on behalf of the poor or making sure that their voices are heard and they can speak up and negotiate for themselves: 'the church has a critical role to play in ensuring that the voices of the poor reverberate in the halls of public policy'.[6] In general, however, advocacy means the churches, from the World Council of Churches (*India*) to local churches, working, again preferably together (*Bangladesh, Colombia, Philippines*), to change the structures and influence the economic and social policies of governments and international institutions so that they are no longer 'skewed against the poor' (*Jamaica* p. 27) but are just and equitable and work in their favour as much as everybody else's. This will not be achieved unless the churches analyse and think carefully before they speak and win over popular

opinion as a necessary backup to their public debating and high level lobbying activities.[7] Every day Christians in local congregations will need to be challenged and encouraged to play their part in national and global campaigns.[8]

Advocate debt forgiveness with rules – Countries should not have to borrow new amounts in order to have their debt forgiven. Debt forgiveness should be tied to free trade which will benefit smaller developing countries. Forgiveness of the debt cannot be conditional on assuming more debt. (*Jamaica* p. 30)

---

7 The issues to be addressed or 'advocated' include the United Nations as an instrument of world governance that seeks the common good (*UN*), human rights violations (*Colombia, India, Palestine*) and corruption.[9] The most frequently mentioned issues have to do with the global economic order: debt,[10] Structural Adjustment Policies, trade and TNCs,[11] employment (*Ghana, Jamaica*) and increasing the aid and development budgets of richer countries (*Bangladesh, Fiji*).

The world-wide ecumenical family of churches ... should contribute towards poverty reduction not only by exposing the unfair practices of multinational companies but also the unfair trade between the developed west and the developing world. For example, multinational companies are using cheap labour, sometimes child labour, to produce goods for supermarkets in developed countries. There are also trade barriers to products from the developing world. While the third world is being forced to open up their markets, those in the west are closing theirs. The world-wide ecumenical family of churches should generate information about these unfair practices and publicize them. In addition they can lobby their governments to ensure that multinational companies do not super-exploit (impoverish) people in the third world. (*Uganda* p. 11)

---

8 Some case studies suggest that advocacy should now take precedence over the more traditional developmental projects and programmes of the churches and even replace them altogether since they cannot tackle poverty fundamentally (*Chile*). Most, whilst recognizing that projects are not enough by themselves and that the churches must go beyond them, show little desire to give them up:[12] 'Be prophetic but don't give up relief work and development projects' (*Jamaica* p. 27)

might be a fairly generally held view. The recommendation is therefore a 'both – and' rather than an 'either – or'.

9 Where projects and programmes are continued the approach should not be piecemeal (*Chile*) but prioritized and part of long-term strategies (*Russia, LABOUR*). They should empower rather than perpetuate dependency (*Chile, South Africa*). Programme proposals cover the familiar range of age groups from the very young to the elderly (*Bangladesh, Chile*) with women and their needs frequently highlighted.

For a presentation such as ours which has been solicited from women only there often is a tendency for it to be treated as by the way. This can be particularly so, for this project whose original plan was set in the context of Churches. Women are part of the church. The responses of the women we interviewed are not at all 'women's issues' which are out of the main agenda of this project. When women table social concerns, these concerns belong to the broader agenda of all humanity. Illiteracy, poverty, lack of access to healthcare, violence, and under-representation in decision-making circles are societal problems, not women's problems. So, our first recommendation is that, these issues of poverty and wealth which drastically affect the lives of societies, presented here through the eyes of women shall not be relegated to the realm of 'women's issues'. If we do not take action now on these issues, the world agenda in the twenty-first century will not reflect the human reality. (*WORLD YWCA* p. 2)

There is also a long list of issues from credit unions to jobs;[13] but the expected bias towards education, skills and leadership training, and healthcare re-emerges.[14] *Philippines* describes the education programmes needed as 'massive' (p. 16).

Educate as well as send 'barrels.' (*Jamaica* p. 29)

Whatever the programme, it is important to assess it and to use only methodologies and techniques that have been tried and tested and have proved themselves effective (*Chile, Uganda, LABOUR*).

10 Recommendations about relationships are made mostly to the agencies of the so-called Northern churches and recall longstanding discussions about partnership between North and South.[15] In short they call for a greater sense of doing things together as 'equal partners' and 'trusted allies'.[16] Northern agencies should see themselves less as 'donors' and 'enablers' assisting others, and much more as 'participants in a larger

collective effort' (*Chile* p. 33) involving everyone in common problems and shared solutions. This will often mean a greater role for churches and local communities inside poor countries in planning and deciding what is to be done (*Bangladesh, Palestine, Philippines*) and a less dictatorial attitude from agencies (*Philippines*) which should do their best to respect the priorities of the poor, appreciate the difficulties that face them, and adapt to the often slow pace of social change (*Palestine, WORLD YWCA*) rather than insist on bureaucratic deadlines (*Bangladesh*). All sides will be ready to give what they have to give and receive what they lack, whether it is information or money, skills or experience.[17] Whilst there is a long way to go, some case studies acknowledge that more equal partnerships do already exist (*Palestine*). They can be easier to achieve in advocacy work than when it comes to projects and programmes.

Some northern agencies have dealt with some of the Church Related Organizations in Palestine from a basis of inequality. Impatience is often shown to the organizational incapacity of the local organizations that, according to northern partners, lack professionalism and the needed know-how . . . The Church in Palestine, and this is no excuse, is a dying church in terms of numbers of faithful. This, unfortunately, gets reflected on the Church Related Organizations, particularly the local ones. These struggle to witness and to serve but they have problems that need to be worked out: the passing of the torch from old to young; the involvement of women on their boards, decision-making and field work; the activation of different churches' members in their work and the empowerment of the poor themselves throughout the whole process. There is also the traditional rift between clergy and lay people that needs to be surmounted in order to arrive at a common vision and to formulate a society-wide program of action on poverty and on other social and economic ills. These are not easy processes. Hard work is needed. Northern donors and partners need to understand that the Palestinian Church is in specific straits and that while help to upgrade the performance of the Church Related Organizations is a laudable contribution, the road is neither easy nor quick. Time is needed. (*Palestine* p. 33)

---

11 Christian teaching looms large in the recommendations to local churches though it is by no means limited to them.[18] Some believe that a different approach to theology is required as we learn to speak about God not apart from but in the midst of people's sufferings and struggles, difficult as it is. Others talk of the content of theological

and biblical teaching and the need to reconstruct it in the light of people's struggles: a new 'ecumenical theology'? (*South Africa* p. 13). It must overcome the divide between the spiritual and the material, and between prayer and social action. It should reject both poverty and excessive wealth as scandalous and as 'not Kingdom categories', and replace them with what *Jamaica* calls a 'theology of sufficiency' (p. 20). It should awaken Christian congregations and their leaders to the claims of the poor and offer them a faith that sustains their commitment to act against poverty and injustice. *UN*, though it is not alone, is particularly concerned that the churches get their values right.[19] Narrow self-interest, consumerism, materialism, greed, the celebration of growth and wealth accumulation all have to be challenged. The values of volunteerism, generosity, hard work, honesty, stewardship, solidarity, simplicity, of 'being' rather than 'having', must all be upheld.

From today's Colombia, a yet another endless holocaust, we ask ourselves how should we engage a theological task and to which ends? Even more so, we wonder wherever God can be? Could he be in Urabá, or in the provinces of Córdoba, Cesar, Meta, where the horrors of poverty, military actions, displacement of people from their lands, and Human Rights violations permeates the daily lives of their inhabitants? Whatever may God be doing while the actors of violence – the army, police forces, guerrilla, paramilitary, drug traffickers, hired killers, militias, gangs – go around massacring, torturing, threatening, and intimidating helpless civilians? How could we speak of God in the midst of almost two million displaced peasant that come to our cities seeking refuge in the slums of Bogotá, Cali, Medellín, Barranquilla, Barrancabermeja, Villavicencio, Montería?

To take such questions into our hands in order to provide at least an approximate answer is the major challenge that theology has to face in current Colombia. Theology, as understood from a 'traditional point of view', that is, as a discourse about God with no connection whatsoever to the realities out of which it emerges, does not enable the theologian to deal with the aforementioned issues. The traditional theological discourse does not see it fit for a theologian to raise such questions, or else, it lacks the proper methodological tools to discern and take into serious consideration issues of poverty, violence, social and economic injustice, and so forth. Unfortunately, such an allegedly 'Christian Theology' dominates the scene in the Colombian Catholic, Protestant and Pentecostals contexts. (*Colombia* p. 30)

---

12 Sound teaching has then to be communicated.[20] Formation is one very
    important role of the local church. *Germany* calls it 'orientation'. It can
    be achieved through preaching and teaching, study groups, theologi-
    cal education, liturgy and the quality of the community's life together.
    In all these ways values and perspectives are constantly rehearsed and
    kept alive. The churches must not simply 'preach to the converted'
    however but promote these same values in the workplace, in public
    life and in international organizations and institutions like the UN,
    IMF, World Bank and transnational corporations. They must play
    their part in the debate on corporate values and a shared global ethic.

The churches are to be experienced as

  – places of orientation, where questions about the meaning and goal
    of human life and that of society can be kept alive by Christian faith;

  – places of truth and a realistic view of human beings, where fears,
    failure and guilt do not have to be concealed because there is con-
    stant forgiveness and a new beginning for Christ's sake;

  – places of conversion and renewal where people change, notice the
    needs of others and set aside old ways of behaviour;

  – places of solidarity and love of the neighbour, where mutual
    responsibility is affirmed and practised among, and for, one
    another;

  – places of freedom, for discovering that freedom and bonds, self-
    fulfilment and commitment are not opposites but condition one
    another, and that this reciprocal relationship is important for a
    good life;

  – places of hope, for seeking meaningful ways of organizing life
    together in society and looking beyond the present in this quest.
    (*Germany* p. 33)

---

13 Third comes the issue of integrity or credibility.[21] The churches must
    practise what they preach. The values they promote must be upheld
    in their own style of life. What they demand of others they must
    expect of themselves. If they speak out against corruption for example
    then their own procedures must be beyond question. If they campaign
    for decent wages and good working conditions then they must treat
    their own employees likewise. If they have wealth they must use it
    not for self-aggrandizement but to empower the poor.

> How do we talk about these issues in a credible way when we are our-selves part of the affluent world, living on good salaries as UN staff and in various academic positions? Do we not all venture a little dance around the golden calf from time to time? (*UN* p. 23)

14 Much the same point is put, but more attractively, in terms of the local church where it is seen more as a hopeful possibility than a demand.[22] Local churches can be, and are urged to become, 'sites for social and cultural change', where ideals like more equal relations, mutual respect, a simpler lifestyle, having all things in common and solidarity with one another, rich and poor alike, can to some extent be realized. Here hope is not only imagining a different future but actually realizing better ways of living together now. In these circumstances worship can actually turn pain and solitude into solidarity and the celebration of life, and liturgy can be 'part of the work of transformation . . . not a prelude to it' (*LITURGY* p. 17).

> Churches are also privileged sites for social and cultural change (change in group conversations). The celebration of life, solidarity, and restoration in the face of pain, suffering, solitude, or poverty, can take on a profoundly aesthetic and ritualistic, or liturgical, charac-ter. More than an escape from problems, this can be a way of building hope and activating the disposition to personal and collective efforts to overcome poverty. In the same way, churches are also places where it is possible to construct equal relations among genders, gen-erations, ethnicities, minorities, etc., and to incorporate them into the life of the community of faith, as well as to promote such equal re-lations in the lives of each of the people and groups with which the churches relate and interact. (*Chile* p. 30)
>
> The Churches may also encourage the well-to-do among their mem-bers to help as many poor people they can so as to bring the modern Church close to the Nature of the New Testament Church where they had all their things in common such that there was no one in need. (*Ghana* p. 32)

7

COMBATING POVERTY AND GREED

In conclusion, recurring emphases are noted and reaffirmed. A five-point programme is put forward involving: focusing on excessive wealth; putting advocacy on an equal footing with development programmes; building a global alliance; honouring and resourcing local churches; clarifying an ecumenical theology of poverty, wealth and justice. 2015 targets for the churches are proposed.

1 In March 2002 the 24 case study writers met in Ghana for the last time to decide what they now most wanted to say together.

Recurring emphases

2 Looking back over the case studies they noted a number of recurring emphases so giving a slightly more 'quantitative' rather than 'qualitative' edge to their findings. Put briefly those emphases are as follows.

  (i) The outlook for the poor is gloomy. Poverty is still a dominating feature of our world and the gap between rich and poor is getting wider. Whilst there have been changes for the better, for many their situation grows worse and leads to a mood of despair.

 (ii) Women, despite their pivotal role in family, social and economic life, are often the most disadvantaged and, along with their children, especially vulnerable.

(iii) Poverty has many dimensions: material, social, psychological and spiritual. It is characterized above all by lack of employment, income and power. It is accompanied by social disintegration, conflict, disease, uprootedness, and an environment exhausted by the rich as much as the poor.

(iv) There are many causes of poverty. Prominent among them are the economic system, corruption and bad governance and, in many countries still, the unequal distribution of land. Poverty is to some extent self-perpetuating. Poverty and the gap between rich and poor provoke conflict for example and conflict makes poor people even poorer.

 (v) The effects of the global economy and its neo-liberal policies on the poor are largely negative.

(vi) Excessive wealth, in many ways the reverse of poverty and its causes, is as much of a problem as poverty itself.

(vii) The teaching of the churches with their 'spiritualizing' and 'prosperity' gospels, their theologies of 'liberation' and more 'holistic' approaches is varied and often confusing. Some leaders and teachers say little about injustice and fail to encourage Christian action beyond acts of charity and kindness.

(viii) Nevertheless there are many inspiring stories to tell about the work of the churches and their agencies in response to poverty, including acts of charity, emergency aid, welfare services, developmental projects and programmes, and advocacy. Advocacy work tends to be weaker than the rest but is growing stronger.

(ix) Education and training are regarded as very important ways to overcome poverty and feature strongly in church activities. There is a similar emphasis on job creation, income generation and healthcare.

(x) There are three fundamental keys to overcoming poverty. One is a changed relationship with poor people, their communities and organizations, acknowledging and respecting their strengths, sharing with them in decision-making and providing them with equal opportunities to resolve their own problems. The second is promoting good governance on behalf of the poor, based on their economic, social and cultural rights. The third is a reformed economic system with a better distribution of wealth and more equal opportunities for everyone to earn a living.

(xi) The churches and their organizations, separately and together with civil society, and individual church members in their daily life and work are called to contribute to all three. It will require them to act and advocate as respectful partners in strong alliances.

Challenging the churches to combat poverty and greed

3 Having noted and reaffirmed these recurring emphases the case study writers agreed on five priorities for the churches. Taken together they could be seen as a Programme to Combat Poverty and Greed which the churches might adopt for the next few years of the early twenty-first century. They have to do with:

Excessive Wealth and Greed
Advocacy Projects and Programmes
A Global Alliance

Honouring and Resourcing the Local Church
An Ecumenical Theology of Poverty, Wealth and Justice

To draw attention to excessive wealth and greed as well as poverty

4 There are a number of reasons for turning the spotlight on excessive wealth. It is contrary to gospel teaching. It is not a separate issue from poverty but in many respects the same issue. They have common causes and integrally related characteristics: the ability of the rich to earn a living for example is the inability of the poor; the strength of the rich is the weakness of the poor. Worse still, excessive wealth is itself a cause of poverty. The drive to create a rising tide of wealth and become rich does not benefit rich and poor alike so that 'all the boats rise'. It does not bring an end to poverty but often exacerbates it. And by concentrating only on poverty attention is deflected from the rich. At most they are seen as the possible source of a solution to poverty. They are not seen as a major part of the problem.

Having recognized the importance of the issue, the Project did not get very far in addressing it. One presentation was made at the New Delhi Colloquium on the biblical teaching on wealth. Excessive wealth, seen largely as the accumulation of material possessions and power by a privileged few, while so many others lived in poverty, was described as 'sinful', 'shameful and scandalous'. The Old Testament prophets and the teachings of Jesus warn against it. Money leads to misplaced loyalties; it usurps the place of God; the love of it is the root of all evil (1 Timothy 6.10).

Can excessive wealth be defined as concretely as we sometimes define poverty? Is there a wealth line above which no one should rise just as there is a poverty line below which no one should be allowed to fall? Can we speak of 'relative wealth' in the way we speak of 'relative poverty' so focusing once again on the unacceptable disparities within countries and communities, rich or poor, as well as between them? What might be the indicators of excessive wealth to stand alongside poverty indicators like income per capita for example, or infant mortality rates, when governments and international institutions are encouraged to monitor and report on both?

There are hints in the case studies at a more acceptable understanding of wealth. It is 'holistic' in that it involves spiritual, social and cultural as well as material wealth. It is seen as a gift from God calling for thanksgiving, stewardship and tithing. It is shared and generous, particularly towards the most vulnerable. It is sustainable and does not impoverish the earth.

A culture in which greed and the endless accumulation of material possessions are regarded as normal and legitimate has to be eroded by alternative values such as self-restraint, simplicity, a sense of proportion, justice, generosity, volunteerism (a 'giving culture'), holism and greater discernment as to 'means' and 'ends'.

The integrity of the churches also needs examining. They are inevitably involved in the culture of greed and the systems that encourage it. They often collude with them and benefit from them. They contain within their own life the same disparities between rich and poor people and congregations.

A good deal of hard-headed thinking and research needs to be done however if excessive wealth is to be tackled effectively. Moral appeals to the rich and attempts to change the culture will not be enough by themselves. 'Second-order issues' in all their complexity now come to the fore such as the role of free enterprise, competition and self-interest in driving a successful economy; and whether excessive wealth is ever acquired legitimately (by hard work, 'fair play' or inheritance for example) or only, as the Project has implied, dishonestly or by exploitation. Due weight must also be given to the intimate connection between wealth and power and the fact that neither are usually given up or shared with others, or knowingly put in jeopardy by those who possess them. If 'excessive wealth' and 'poverty' are to be replaced by the 'commonweal' or by 'common well-being' it will require the levers of international law based on human rights, economic treaties and trade rules, and a developing understanding of 'enlightened self-interest' or 'the common good', not just appeals to the generosity and sense of fair play of wealthy people and nations. There must be the rule of justice, not just the plea for it.

To put advocacy on a more equal footing with projects and programmes

5 The churches seem unanimous in their ongoing commitment to deliver services and promote community development through projects and programmes. The case studies reveal no inclination to give them up and say little about systematic attempts at evaluation (though these are known to exist). Clearly such programmes have a necessary part to play, whether charitable, diaconal or developmental. The relevance of education and training for example is obvious.

The rationale for projects and programmes needs however to be stated afresh. What are they thought to achieve? By what criteria are they evaluated? How do they contribute to fundamental change as well as, quite rightly, supporting the poor while that change is brought about? What is required in terms of co-ordination and strategy to make them a real force to be reckoned with? For what reasons do we need both advocacy and the more traditional projects and programmes? (AIDS might be used as a good illustration of the point, requiring as it does advocacy on, say, pharmaceutical manufacturing and supply but also educational programmes, medical care and social services.) How can the two be more firmly integrated: advocacy as part of programmes and programmes as springboards for advocacy?

Advocacy receives less attention and resources from the churches than projects and programmes (though it is gaining ground and some of their organizations, such as APRODEV and the Ecumenical Advocacy Alliance, exist mainly for advocacy purposes). Advocacy is of crucial importance. In terms of combating poverty it recognizes and addresses the fundamental issues. Whether we are talking about the outside resources and support systems which in the end no community or community development programme can do without, or the lack of income and lack of power that lie at the root of any person's poverty, the key issues have to do with good governance and equitable economic systems. If these are to be changed it requires the churches along with others to raise their voices and lobby and campaign for change. Some case studies suggest that advocacy should now supersede projects and programmes altogether. Most accept the need for them to continue; but no amount of ongoing support for poor people in the form of community programmes can be justified if, at the same time, bringing about fundamental, structural change, both social and economic, is not given at least equal attention. Programmes and advocacy must go together.

To build a strong and effective global alliance to combat poverty and greed

6 The gathering strength of the global economy and its negative consequences (described in one case study as 'the forces of death') call for an organized countervailing power for life or what was described as the 'globalization of solidarity'. Its voice would be prophetic, drawing on biblical faith. Building on many existing networks as well as encouraging new ones, it would create a global alliance against poverty,

greed and injustice. It would be inclusive, coherent, effective and well informed.

This alliance would expose and challenge global economic policies. It would look for alternatives and campaign for reform. It would take up issues such as trade, governance, sustainability and the creation and distribution of wealth and opportunity, but always with the unjust disparities between rich and poor as its core agenda. It would engage with the international financial institutions (World Bank, International Monetary Fund and regional development banks) and the World Trade Organization, with transnational corporations, the United Nations, governments and regional economic blocs.

One great strength of this (Jubilee?) alliance would be its inclusiveness. It would take seriously local churches and communities (as did the Jubilee 2000 Campaign) as well as national, regional and international church bodies and organizations, linking them together: local with global, 'South–South', North, South, East and West, making everyone feel part of one community. The churches, properly mobilized, are one of the largest 'NGOs' in the world with huge potential in the struggle for justice.

The alliance would also include many issues, approaches and networks while bringing to them a sense of coherence and mutual reinforcement by providing a shared policy framework and a common strategy for action.

The alliance would need to establish an appropriate style of working that was inclusive and effective. Decision-making would be based on respectful relationships between the various constituent members. It would be highly participative whilst providing decisive leadership. It would be efficient but not overwhelmed by bureaucracy. It would make good use of information technology made available to all. If we need to strengthen solidarity, we need to learn to 'manage solidarity' well.

The alliance and its members would need to be well briefed. Both within and beyond the churches and their agencies there are already many institutions researching and analysing issues related to poverty and inequality, evaluating existing policies and proposing new ones. There is no suggestion that yet more should be created. It is essential however that existing research and analysis is collected, digested, related to the Christian faith and then made available to the churches in appropriate forms so that whether lobbying and campaigning at a local or global level their arguments and proposals are well informed. The formation of a network of existing church-related research institutions could be a significant step towards achieving this.

Examples of where such information is required in a 'usable' form include: human rights issues; the inter-related causes of poverty; existing and alternative policies relating to global capitalism (e.g. the second-order questions on debt, trade, corporate responsibility, etc., already referred to); evaluations and models of good practice in development programmes and campaigning; country, regional and global priorities and strategies.

One source of information for the churches could be a World Church Report on Poverty and Wealth along the lines of this 'prototype' produced every five years or so. It could provide them with an overall picture, a shared strategic framework in which to act and advocate in their various ways, a means of evaluating progress, and a stimulus to action.

Other forms of useful information could be: country case studies building on the methodology of 'Project 21' for use by outside and in-country agencies (as shared country strategy papers); stories of good practice; and briefing papers on specific topics.

It is of course important for the churches and their members to participate in even wider networks (e.g. of other faiths and other movements within civil society) and strategies (like the Millennium Development Goals aimed at cutting poverty in half and Poverty Reduction Strategies). Churches must join hands with all men and women of good will. This does not always prove easy. The churches may lack confidence. Governments may exclude them. The churches' visibility can be lost. A strong alliance of churches themselves should therefore be a step towards more effective engagement on a wider front but not a way of withdrawing from it.

The recently formed Ecumenical Advocacy Alliance based in Geneva, and the World Council of Churches, could be focal points for developing the kind of inclusive and effective alliance which is required if the churches are to meet the challenges of globalization.

To strengthen and renew local churches and (Christian) communities to combat poverty and greed and promote social transformation

7 Poor people and countries should be the 'subjects' and not 'objects' of the struggle for justice. They are as wise and capable as 'outsiders', often more so. They should not be dictated to but respected and sup-

ported in tackling poverty and inequality in the ways they believe are best. National and global strategies are necessary, but so is a whole variety of local initiatives, complementing each other and contributing to the whole. One case study (*Germany*) referred to the principle of 'subsidiarity' which insists on keeping decision-making at the appropriate level with a bias towards the 'lower' or local level rather than the higher one. Local communities should decide more often than they do. They should be strengthened from without but not over-ruled.

Local communities can be strengthened from without in many ways. Outside funding can help. Barriers (including legal, economic, political, cultural, and infrastructural barriers) to local initiatives can be removed by way of access to credit and land for example and by increased participation. Social capital can be built up through better healthcare, education and training (for income generation), leadership development and targeted support for women.

Local church congregations are part, sometimes the major part, of these local communities. They should not be by-passed or underestimated by the churches and their organizations as they combat poverty and greed but should be strengthened and renewed to be full participants.

For not a few (and it applies equally to rich congregations as well as poor, and sometimes more so) this will require a different understanding of their mission and ministry. They must offer the hope of new life not only to individuals drawn into their ranks but to the whole community as well. They must build up not only the capacity of the church but also the capacity of the community that it exists to serve. They must not only do their own distinctive work of sharing the gospel but join hands with the social groups and movements around them to work with all people of good will for the good of everyone. The training institutions of the churches and their wider specialized ministries can help to bring these changes about.

If congregations and church members, whether poor or rich, are to promote social transformation and cope with the heavy demands it will make on them, they will need to experience their local churches as places which do not only speak to them about their duties and obligations but also inspire, equip and support them in what they are called to do.

Liturgy could play a highly supportive and formative role (according to the case study on the topic). It needs to be rooted in the local (indigenous music, song and story for example reflecting the day-to-day context – as strikingly illustrated by the daily worship at the

Colloquium in New Delhi in November 2000 where the reality of conflict and violence came very much to the fore) and reflect more often than it does the gospel of good news to the poor.

Clear and adequate biblical and theological teaching, accompanied by appropriate educational materials, on poverty, wealth and justice, are needed at all levels (e.g. ministerial and congregational training) to build up the kind of faith and spirituality which will undergird political action and discipleship and counteract the influence of more conservative, prosperity-based and spiritualizing theologies.

Teaching and training will need to go even further. Congregations need to be far better briefed on issues relating to poverty and wealth (such as globalization, ecology, trade and debt) and the policies of their governments and how these can be influenced by local people as 'political disciples'.

And, if Christians are to go against the public culture of excessive wealth and greed, they should find within the church a developing counter-culture or lifestyle marked by equal respect (not least between women and men), self-restraint, tithing, generosity, justice, integrity and 'holistic wealth', providing them with a quite different but positive orientation. Congregations should be 'sites' of transformation in themselves. They will need to be 'with' and not just 'for' the poor.

Should a Sunday be set aside by the World Church, perhaps to coincide with the United Nations International Day for the Eradication of Poverty, in October, with liturgical and educational materials provided, to recall the churches in every place to what, according to the gospel, always lies at the heart of their mission and close to the heart of God? The churches certainly need ways of challenging and sustaining each other. Many have found the 'twinning' of congregations and churches from all round the world, especially across the divides of poverty and wealth, a helpful expression of practical solidarity.

To clarify an ecumenical theology of poverty, wealth and justice

8 If there is to be a renewed and strengthened solidarity between the churches it will need to be rooted in a clear and emphatic faith which they all share. This unity and faith will not be achieved easily in the light of the confusion and variety of teaching revealed by the case studies. It will be doubly difficult in a pluralist and relativist culture where any such teaching easily falls under the (hermeneutical) suspicion of serving the vested interests of those who teach it, rich and

poor alike. It is true that no teachings can escape the influence of our human limitations and perversities. They will always be partial, never absolute. The worst forms of partiality can however be avoided by people with different interests and outlooks, such as rich and poor, women and men, North and South, talking together though well aware that with the best will in the world such conversations are difficult whilst power is unequal. On the evidence of the Project, some meeting of minds across differences is possible. In any case, as mature human beings, we are required to make up our minds and adopt the most adequate point of view we can reach and act upon it without denying its inevitable shortcomings. We have to be decisive and 'opinionated' but also modest and undogmatic, highly committed but also reflective at one and the same time.

When it comes to the substance of a clearer ecumenical theology, the case study writers unanimously turn their backs on the so-called 'spiritualizing' and 'prosperity' gospels in favour of the common ground shared by liberation theology and what was referred to as a more holistic approach (see chapter 3). For them justice for the poor is central to the gospel and the church's mission; redemption is material and spiritual, personal and structural, individual and social, and involves all creation. This gospel is unequivocal in its opposition to a world ruled by Mammon and not by God. The churches must be equally emphatic. The reality we now face, of growing poverty, inequality and greed, is not only scandalous but sinful. It is not what Christ died to achieve. He came to proclaim good news to the poor. He speaks of repentance and forgiveness to both rich and poor alike. His Kingdom is a vision of life in all its fullness – of God's generous abundance shared by all. Christ calls us to renewed commitment to work with him to bring it about. He inspires in us the hope of the gospel. His resurrection affirms that the forces for life are stronger than the forces of death. He says to us: 'Behold! I am making all things new!' (Revelation 21.5).

Teaching along such lines as these needs to be more carefully worked out, not in the abstract but whilst actually engaging with the struggle against poverty and greed, and then made accessible and winningly expounded to clarify the thinking and inspire the confidence of the churches.

2015 goals for the churches

9 The world at large has set itself a number of Millennium Development Goals sometimes referred to as '2015 targets' aimed to cut poverty in

'2015 Millennium Goals' for the Churches

1 **Share liturgies and create new ones which engage with the realities of wealth and poverty** and
2 **Provide clear and accessible teaching and educational programmes on Christianity, poverty and wealth and on the economic order** so that congregations are inspired and equipped to engage in structural change and bring about God's justice.
3 **Define a 'greed line' to stand alongside the 'poverty line'** in each country, translating Gospel teaching on wealth into concrete and contemporary guidance for Christians.
4 **Organize a World Church Sunday on Poverty and Wealth** in October to coincide with the UN International Day for the Eradication of Poverty to focus the attention of the churches on their calling to overcome greed and poverty.
5 **Re-examine the reasons for supporting poverty-related projects and programmes** to make sure they are advocates of fundamental structural change in favour of the poorest.
6 **Give priority to local churches and communities** in resourcing and decision-making.
7 **Participate in national poverty reduction strategies** in every country so that the churches make their full contribution to policy-making, implementation and monitoring.
8 **Support and actively participate in an inclusive global alliance of the churches** and their organizations (focused on the Ecumenical Advocacy Alliance) to 'globalize solidarity' and make church advocacy more effective.
9 **Create an ecumenical network of research institutions** to exchange and co-ordinate their findings on advocacy issues and make them available to the churches.
10 **Produce a World Church Report on Poverty and Wealth in 2007 and 2015** to provide a framework within which the varied activities of the churches can gain greater coherence and reinforce each other.

half. Should the churches set '2015 goals' of their own which will put them in a stronger position to help achieve the Millennium Development Goals and bring about God's justice in many other ways as well? The case study writers believe that they should and made the ten proposals on the previous page. They arose out of their five priorities, and are addressed to the churches and their organizations at all the different levels of their life, from the local to the international, for them to take up in their own appropriate ways. A World Church Report on Poverty and Wealth for example (see goal 10) may need to be sponsored by a body like the World Council of Churches or the Ecumenical Advocacy Alliance, but many churches and organizations can contribute to it as they have done to this 'prototype'; even local churches can help with monitoring and evaluating on the ground. Or again, liturgies and Christian education (see goals 1 and 2) belong to local congregations but will draw on the wider experience and expertise of their national churches.

10 Finally, what are the five-point Programme to Combat Poverty and Greed and its 2015 targets expected to achieve? What hope is there of a brighter future, especially for the poor? The case study writers acknowledged that there was a good deal of pessimism. Many of those they had talked to expected to see a worsening situation with mounting poverty and unemployment, daily violence and social disintegration. Others were cautious and spoke only of what they would like to happen rather than what they expected to happen, whether it was important but mundane improvements to roads and housing or a church renewed and orienting its members towards justice issues, or a world transformed by a vision of God's Shalom. Still others said little or nothing about future hopes as if present tasks were enough.

The case study writers spoke of their own continuing grounds for hope in the gospel of Jesus Christ with its good news for the poor, its invitations and challenges to the rich, and its proclamation of the coming of God's Kingdom. They also spoke of the 'reservoir of decency' (*LABOUR, UN*) within all human beings, reflecting the image of God.

And the Project itself, or rather the endeavours of the countless communities and individuals it had heard about and then described, represented for them another kind of hope: that if we cannot fashion a perfectly just world, even with God, we can always make this world more just and healthy than it is. It is open to change. More good can always be achieved by intelligent love. God believes the world and its peoples have potential and so do we. Our commitment to each other and to the God of the poor will always be worthwhile. There is point in strategizing for a future and committing ourselves to a programme to combat poverty and greed. Some words from Namibia reflected their mood:

> It is important that we focus on the small bright lights of hope. Africans are at least beginning to direct the course of their destiny. In the global arena it is a renaissance that must mean that Africa refuses to be a passive onlooker in a changing world, a hapless victim to modern machinations of the forces historically responsible for her woes. For Africans, the African renaissance is a reawakening of the giant from the deep slumber of official corruption, criminal neglect of social responsibility and misrule by African rulers. In Africa we have realized that the very fact of resistance in the face of very powerful forces of evil is a small bright light of hope. (*Namibia* p. 21)

8

THE STORY OF 'PROJECT 21'

1 'Project 21' began in 1997. It was initiated by the Association of World Council of Churches related Development Organizations in Europe (APRODEV) in consultation with the WCC but was soon owned and directed by the participants themselves.

2 The purpose of the study was to see how best the churches, their organizations and agencies could respond to poverty and wealth in the early years of the twenty-first century. These issues had of course been on the churches' agenda from the outset but they became increasingly prominent on the ecumenical agenda with the growing presence and influence of the churches of the South. From the 1940s onwards there was a great flowering of inter-church aid, service to refugees and development work.[1] Towards the end of the twentieth century, however, world events left the ecumenical family less certain about how best to tackle world poverty. The word 'globalization' was now on everybody's lips. The Cold War had come to an end but conflict had not. Capitalism was said to have 'triumphed' over socialism. Ideological debate often gave way to pragmatic approaches. The effects of neo-liberal economic policies and technological developments especially in information technology were all pervasive. Meanwhile poverty persisted. There seemed to be more questions than answers.

3 In 1993 four European-based ecumenical agencies (Christian Aid in the UK, Interchurch Organization for Development Cooperation (ICCO) in Holland, Bread for the World, The Protestant Association for Co-operation in Development (EZE) in Germany), with the help of 'partners' in developing countries, made an attempt at 'Discerning the Way Together'[2] in order to clarify policies for the future, but they soon recognized the need to go further and be more inclusive. The turn of the century, with its accompanying hopes and fears, seemed a good moment to do so and, if possible, to reinvigorate the debate about the ecumenical response to poverty.

4 The process that these agencies and the WCC then initiated was nick-named 'Project 21'. It was originally intended to involve the symbolic

number of 21 countries representing North, South, East and West as they entered the twenty-first century.

As a first step a Steering Group called together by APRODEV and the WCC[3] agreed to consult as best they could with friends and colleagues in their regions, explaining to them what they had in mind and inviting a number of potential case study writers (preferably under 45 years of age) to a meeting in October 1999 at High Leigh, Hoddesdon, UK.

Nineteen people accepted the invitation and agreed to be part of the Project. Subsequently other names were added making a total of 24 case studies. Nineteen were country-based[4] and five were more focused studies:[5] on the particularly disadvantaged position of women in poverty (World YWCA); on church worship and liturgy and how these took account of poverty and justice issues; and on the roles played by labour movements especially in Brazil, transnational corporations (Norwegian Church Aid) and the United Nations (Danchurchaid).

At High Leigh all the case study writers agreed to work to a similar brief so that we could more easily compare one country with another and make connections. They would all seek the support of their national ecumenical organizations and bring together a reference group to ensure that as far as possible their findings were not personal to themselves but more widely representative. They would all adopt a highly consultative approach that was both ecumenical and inter-disciplinary and drew on the insights of economists, politicians, social scientists, industrialists and development workers as well as theologians. They would all try to meet the same seven constituencies in their countries and talk through with them the same series of questions.

The seven constituencies were:

rich and
poor people in church congregations and communities
government officials
academics
non-governmental organizations (NGOs)
church leaders
the private sector.

The questions had to do with: how poverty and wealth were experienced and understood in their countries (see chapter 1), what were the causes were (chapter 2), how they were related to Christian teaching and the mission and work of the churches (chapter 3), what practical actions were being taken (chapters 4 and 5) and what were regarded as the most appropriate responses the churches and their organizations should make to these issues in the early years of the twenty-first century (chapter 6).

Their findings would then be written up under the same headings and the papers completed and copied to all participants to form the basic working documents for a colloquium which would be held in New Delhi, India in November 2000. Before that most of the case study writers were able to attend a second meeting in Copenhagen in the Spring of 2000 when they reported on the progress they had made, adjusted the process in the light of their experiences and made plans for the New Delhi Colloquium.

5 There was a remarkable degree of success in achieving comparability between the papers but also a determination to respect the obvious differences between countries and the need for people to work in their own ways. All situations are unique, but some seemed more distinctive than others: Colombia (drug trafficking and conflict), Germany (East–West unification), South Korea (crisis of 1997), Fiji (crisis of 2000) and Palestine (Arab–Israeli conflict) were obvious examples; and in some cases circumstances made it difficult to complete the work along the agreed lines. Nevertheless almost all the studies were completed and made available to all participants two months before the New Delhi Colloquium so that participants could read and reflect on them before meeting together. Despite the differences, shared insights began to emerge.

Some studies involved large numbers of people: over 400 in Chile, 200 in Colombia and more than 2,500 in Germany. The World YWCA drew on material from 13 countries. Two studies were the work of small groups: a group of twelve for the UN study, for example, and five for Liturgy. The paper from South Africa focused on a single settlement: Etwatwa, wholly inhabited by black Africans.

Inevitably contacts with the seven constituencies were uneven. It could be difficult to talk with government officials, the private sector and extremely wealthy people, though their voices can be heard. Responses to some of the questions were weak. Little was said about new and promising initiatives being taken or planned by churches and agencies to combat poverty and excessive wealth, and almost nothing was said about how the churches intended to evaluate their work. The weakness may of course lie with the questioning.

6 The vast majority of the case study writers worked heroically in English, their second or even third language, both when writing up their

papers and when discussing them and the Project at our meetings in New Delhi and elsewhere.

7 Almost half the time in New Delhi (five working days) was spent in small working groups critiquing the case study papers and drawing up an agenda of issues for discussion in plenary and proposals for subsequent action. Fifty-two people came. Each person responsible for a case study was invited to bring with them another person from their country with a different perspective. In addition ecumenical organizations and agencies from both richer and poorer countries sent representatives. In this way it was hoped that many voices would be heard, directly and indirectly, round the table. The Colloquium was further enriched by acts of worship which juxtaposed stories of poverty and wealth (and on almost every occasion conflict as well) from various countries with stories from the Bible. It was hosted by the National Council of Churches in India.

The Colloquium drafted and later revised and agreed a Working Document. It described the project and its participants, their diverse views and areas of agreement. It set out five priorities for the churches for the future which, taken together, could add up to 'A Programme to Combat Poverty and Greed'. They focused on wealth, alliances, and renewing and strengthening local churches for social transformation. Finally the Working Document outlined the continuing work of the Project.

A Prototype World Church Report on Poverty and Wealth

8 One firm decision made in New Delhi was that the Steering Group should make plans to publish a 'prototype' or pilot edition of a World Church Report on Poverty and Wealth by 2002. Such a Report was meant to stand alongside the UNDP Human Development Report and the World Bank World Development Report. It would complement them but make no attempt to ape them. It would be addressed to the churches and their related organizations and agencies especially within the ecumenical family. It would report on:

the churches' current assessments of wealth and poverty
their concrete actions in response
their success and failures
their shared views and goals as well as diversity
their priorities and targets for the immediate and medium-term future.

It was hoped that such a Report would be descriptive and informative and provide the churches with an overall picture to which they could relate their various individual activities, so giving them a greater measure of coherence. The Report might also serve in time as a tool for evaluation, charting the progress made between one edition and another in combating poverty and helping the churches to identify and learn from their achievements and failures. It was strongly felt that the Report should have a prophetic edge which challenged and stimulated the churches to even greater endeavours. Several attempts were made to get a younger theologian from the South to provide it for this one, but the practicalities defeated us.

'Project 21' however could only produce a 'prototype' or an illustration of what we had in mind. It could only float an idea and for obvious reasons. The case study writers were developing a promising way of working within and between their countries and regions but they could not pretend that their research was systematic or comprehensive enough, or that the number of countries and churches involved was anything like sufficient, to justify the title of a *World* Church Report. North America was not represented, again due to practical difficulties. Some case study writers were Roman Catholic and the Roman Catholic Church was referred to in several studies but it was not formally involved in the Project. The special studies suffered from similar shortcomings. If it was important to hear Christian voices from inside the five sectors and institutions chosen it was equally important to do so from inside others such as the World Bank and the IMF. The gaps were all too plain. But maybe the work that had been done and the way of working that had been developed would be sufficiently promising to persuade the ecumenical family, including the Ecumenical Advocacy Alliance, to build on our idea and take steps to produce more adequate reports in the future, say every 5 years, with perhaps contributory studies on particular issues during the interim period. If they did, it might do much to enable the multitude of churches, national and local, round the world to pull together more effectively whilst acting in different ways, so realizing their potential as one of the world's most powerful NGO networks and tackling one of the central concerns of the gospel: to bring good news to the poor.

After the Colloquium in New Delhi in 2000 much of the work of 'Project 21' concentrated on preparing the prototype World Church Report on poverty and wealth for publication and on producing a video to accompany it. Every case study writer was asked to revise their paper in the light of the discussions in New Delhi using a common check list and an individual critique of each paper. Some were able to respond to this request more thoroughly than others. The revised case studies together with the Working Document from the New Delhi Colloquium then became the basis for a draft 'prototype' which in turn became the text which the case study writers and the Steering Group worked on at their final meeting in March 2002. Without pretending there was complete unanimity, all of chapters 1–8, written up by the Director of the Project, have their general support and agreement.

One of the ways in which this prototype Report differs from those of the UN and the World Bank is that, for the most part, it avoids quoting the kind of statistics which feature prominently and are so important and necessary for their purposes. Instead, the Report favours a different set of primary data, namely the voices of actual people and especially the voices of the poor. Some of those voices are directly quoted. Often their identities are made clear and the constituencies from which they come. But not always so. At times, for example in chapter 3 about Christian teaching, the question 'Who is speaking?' is not easy to answer. Is it a constituency voice or is it the voice of the reference group? Does it reflect what people actually think or what a reference group believes they ought to think? Generally the voices are from within church circles and despite some areas of uncertainty the Report can claim to be a fairly reliable piece of 'qualitative' if not 'quantitative' research. It presents a comprehensive range of views even if it cannot always be precise about who has expressed them on any particular occasion, or be certain as to how many people hold them. It reports on the range of opinions but less on the balance of opinion.

9　In gathering together the often rich and always varied material from the case studies it has been difficult at times to avoid catalogues, not to say endless catalogues, of opinions, actions and proposals without jeopardizing the claim that the outcome is a reliable piece of qualitative research and without going back on the commitment of the Project to respect differences and detail whilst searching for comparability and agreement. No opinions or material have been included in chapters 1–6 which cannot be found in the 24 case studies as revised and completed by August 2001 (and before 11 September). Chapter 7, on the other hand, goes a little beyond them at times and incorporates views of the case study writers as expressed at their final meeting in Ghana in March 2002.

Evaluation

10 The meeting in Ghana not only finalized the Project and its conclusions; it also spent time evaluating the Project, in so far as that was possible at such close quarters.

Some of its limitations have already been referred to. One of the more serious may well be a lack of engagement with those who advocate neo-liberal policies as the best hope of the poor.

The shortage of explicit references to conflict and violence was surprising given the countries which had been studied (Colombia and Palestine for example), the many forms it takes (including social, structural, religious, domestic as well as military violence), its intimate links with economic order and disorder, and the power it has to make people rich and keep people poor.

The methodology, on the other hand, won warm approval. The international team of 24, their meetings together and their shared way of working had been supportive. Differences had been respected. The method of researching and writing the case studies in each country seemed promising. To some extent it had included poorer communities and given them a platform in line with the Report's own recommendations. It could be built on and used to produce joint country strategy papers for agencies and others (such as NGOs, people's organizations and government departments) to share, so encouraging the more co-operative and strategic approach that many felt was needed (see chapter 6 section 4). Such strategy papers could then engage with the Poverty Reduction Strategy Papers required by the World Bank and the debt cancellation process.

Grass roots people and communities had been listened to and taken seriously.

There had been an encouraging attempt to link the perspectives of local people with those of national and international institutions (like the United Nations and transnational corporations), and the different geographical areas: North, South, East and West in a more inclusive discussion.

A wide range of opinion within the churches had been carefully recorded and distilled in a useful piece of qualitative research.

11 Serious questions however were raised. Had the Project achieved what it set out to achieve? Had it taken the world of the early twenty-first century fully into account? Had the events of 11 September 2001 made the case study work, done before then, look out of touch? Had the Project with its Report and recommendations contributed

anything fresh to the ongoing debate about the churches' response to poverty and wealth, or was it still largely trapped in the old familiar ecumenical debates of the past? Had it anything 'new' to say which had not been said before? Were the proposals sufficiently radical or prophetic? Had they any cutting edge? Had enough attention been given to following them through and finding an institutional base for further work?

By way of reply, the Project had produced a number of insights and emphases which seemed 'fresh' if not entirely 'new'.

- (i) It had turned the spotlight very deliberately on excessive wealth as well as greed.
- (ii) It produced its findings out of a much more inclusive process or 'methodology' than is often the case, involving the local, national and international, North and South and many disciplines and constituencies.
- (iii) It hinted strongly at the need for a wider 'ecumenism' than the churches, involving many faiths, cultures and ideologies seeking shared ethical values and making common cause for the common good.
- (iv) It highlighted the need for an inclusive global advocacy alliance.
- (v) It reflected a new sense of urgency in the face of growing despair, which requires strengthened commitment and solidarity.
- (vi) It provided a fresh overview of church teaching and practice on poverty and wealth.

12 A great deal in the case studies and this Report nevertheless looks familiar, for example:

- (i) the longstanding antagonism to global capitalism in ecumenical circles;
- (ii) the continuing emphasis on developmental projects and programmes however well co-ordinated;
- (iii) the feeling of local congregations that they are undervalued and often by-passed or side-lined in the development process;
- (iv) a continuation of the old arguments about a more equal 'partnership' and 'resource-sharing' between North and South, to replace the overbearing attitude of 'donor' agencies;
- (v) a long list of important issues to be addressed from debt and trade to AIDS, conflict and uprooted people, that are well established on the ecumenical agenda.

13 Even if the Report did do little more than highlight familiar issues that would not, it was felt, necessarily provide grounds for criticism, and for several reasons. First, these old debating points and issues might

still be valid. Second, the 'newness' of the world at the beginning of the twenty-first century can be exaggerated as can the 'newness' of the world after 11 September 2001. The events associated with that day and its aftermath certainly brought a number of poverty-related issues to the fore. One was an increase in military budgets and the fear that it would lead to a corresponding decrease of resources available for poverty reduction. Another was the need for alliances against poverty and greed between people of all religious faiths and none. But in many respects those events highlighted long existing problems rather than new ones. They have to do with poverty, the countless deaths of innocent but terrorized people, and the deep sense of injustice at the growing divisions between rich and poor. They do not justify violence and terrorism and Christians must continue to promote non-violent ways to seek justice (as for example in the ecumenical Decade to Overcome Violence). But although they never justify violence and terrorism, poverty and injustice do become their fertile breeding ground. The broad solutions therefore remain much the same and 11 September underlines the urgency of reports like this one and its conclusions rather than throwing them into doubt. What is still required now as before is national and international governance on behalf of all, including the poorest, based on human rights, and an economic system marked by a fairer distribution of wealth and more equal opportunities for poor countries and poorer workers to earn a living. Even at this broad level there are no universal solutions. Good governance and just and workable economic systems are not the same in every place; and such structural changes take time. Far from looking for the 'new' what the gospel may require of us is persistence and patience in already known tasks. When one representative of the churches in the North commented at the New Delhi Colloquium that 'there is nothing new in all of this; we've discussed it all before', the pained but courteous reply from the South was that what were 'tired old issues' for some were still daily realities and matters of life and death for others, and no one's record of overcoming them was all that impressive.

14 That having been said, it was recognized that the world has obviously changed since the churches and their organizations settled into their familiar policies and practices in the latter part of the twentieth century. Globalization has made a difference. The end of the Cold War and now the beginning of the 'War against Terrorism' have made a difference. The 'triumph of capitalism' and the all-pervasive effects of neo-liberal economic policies have made a difference. What is not so very different

is the depth and extent of poverty. However justified in some respects, it may not therefore be sufficient simply to repeat what the churches have long been saying or to report that they see no particular reason to stop doing what they are doing; which is why there are real grounds for concern that two of the questions put to the seven constituencies in the 19 country-based case studies produced little or nothing by way of reply. One question asked what new and promising initiatives to combat poverty were being planned by the churches. The other asked how the churches intended to evaluate what they were doing in order to learn from their successes and failures and be more effective in the future. The lack of questioning of existing practices and the dearth of new ideas were worrying faced with the fact that present church practices do not apparently meet with all that much success.

15 Two other omissions from this Report were recognized as giving cause for concern. The global neo-liberal economy was either hotly rejected or said to be in need of reform. Where it was rejected no suggestions were made as to what an alternative economic system would look like. Where it was said to be in need of reform *Germany* was a strong advocate for the social market, and the case study on *TNCs* for corporate social responsibility. They reflected and tried to structure into the economic system the widespread concern for a fairer distribution of wealth and opportunity so that the economy becomes less of a battleground for individual gain and more the servant of the common good. In general, however, the case studies had all too little to say about what might be called the 'second order issues' which may well be the real battleground. If, for example, we need good governance of a global market what kind of institutions are needed to give it shape whether at the level of the United Nations or the nation state? If we need fairer trade how are the churches to engage with a round of trade negotiations and the workings of the World Trade Organization? If debt is to be cancelled what are the conditions and mechanisms, and what will prevent a recurrence of the crisis? How will human rights be upheld in international courts of law? What migration rules can allow labour to cross borders and not just capital? What have the churches to contribute to these and many more difficult and detailed issues below the banner headlines?

16 The all-important topic of follow-up was discussed at the Ghana meeting, though not perhaps sufficiently Although many voices had been listened to, 'Project 21' remains the work of 24 case study writers and the people, many in their own countries, they tried to represent. It is not the work of the churches themselves or their organizations or the

European agencies which originally agreed to support it. It is nevertheless intended to speak to them about their work and mission. So the
participants fully accepted their ongoing responsibility to see that the
results of their Project were communicated to the churches and their
organizations, often through personal encounters, highlighting the
ways in which any one of them could contribute to implementing its
findings and provide a basis for further work As the '24' try to do so
this publication can be little more than a tool in their hands.

17 It remains to thank all who shared in 'Project 21': the case study writers
who did most of the work often in their second or third language; those
who accompanied them to New Delhi; the Steering Group, Secretary
and Administrator; the APRODEV agencies who funded the Project
but allowed the participants to 'own' it; and all the reference groups
and others who took an interest in what we were doing and cheered
us on. Success or failure of the Project will depend on whether, as a
result of the work done and the suggestions made, the churches' response to poverty and wealth is any more effective in the future than
in the past.

Note: The following documents are available on the Project's website
< http://www.aprodev.net >:

Project Proposal
Briefing Paper (revised version July 1999)
Country Case Studies (19)
Special Studies (5)
Working Document, New Delhi Colloquium 2000

APPENDIX – PARTICIPANTS

Case Study Writers

Monju Baroi	Bangladesh	Samuel Palma	Chile
Ana Mercedes Pereira	Colombia	Aisake Casimira	Fiji
Eberhard Hitzler	Germany	Baffour Dokyi Amoa	Ghana
Kung Lap Yan	Hong Kong	Chandran Paul Martin	India
Theresa Lowe-Ching	Jamaica	Yara Monteiro	LABOUR
Myra Blyth	LITURGY	Hermen Shastri	Malaysia
Paul Isaak `	Namibia	Violeta Rocha	Nicaragua
Bernard Sabella	Palestine	Maureen Loste	Philippines
Vladimir Fedorov	Russia	Molefe Tsele	South Africa
Keum, Joo-Seop	South Korea	Atle Sommerfeldt	TNCs
Bazaara Nyangabyaki	Uganda	Kirsten Lund Larsen	UN
Judy Williams	West Indies	Musimbi Kanyoro	WORLD YWCA

Steering Group

Regional representatives
Samuel Palma
Deenabandhu Manchala
Baffour Dokyi Amoa
Chandran Paul Martin

Ecumenical Advocacy Alliance representative
Linda Hartke

APRODEV representatives
Atle Sommerfeldt
Christian Balslev-Olesen
Eberhard Hitzler

WCC
Myra Blyth
Dr Rogate Mshana

Project Administration

Director	Michael Taylor
Secretary	Rob van Drimmelen
Administrator	Maggie Clay
Media and Video	Martin Cottingham

New Delhi Colloquium Participants

Case Study Writers and Colleagues

Monju Baroi	Bangladesh	James Das	Bangladesh
Sam Palma	Chile	Josefina Hurtado Neira	Chile
Jairo Cruz Hernandez	Colombia	Ana Mercedes Pereira	Columbia
Chantelle Khan	Fiji	Eberhard Hitzler	Germany
Marina Beyer-Grasse	Germany	Baffour Dokyi Amoa	Ghana
Esther Ofei-Aboagye	Ghana	Lap Yan Kung	Hong Kong
Chandran Paul Martin	India	Samuel Jesupatham	India
Theresa Lowe Ching	Jamaica	George Mulrain	Jamaica
Yara Monteiro	LABOUR	Norma Doro	LABOUR
Myra Blyth	LITURGY	Hermen Shastri	Malaysia
Gopala Krishnan	Malaysia	Paul Isaak	Namibia
Enna Van Neel	Namibia	Violeta Rocha	Nicaragua
Ofelia McDavis	Nicaragua	Maureen Loste	Philippines
Vladimir Fedorov	Russia	Marina Chichova	Russia
Khumo Ntlha	South Africa	Keum, Joo-Seop	South Korea
Huh, Chun-Jung	South Korea	Knut Christiansen	TNCs
Hellena Wangusa	Uganda	Kirsten Lund Larsen	UN
Judy Williams	West Indies	Clive Thomas	West Indies
Musimbi Kanyoro	WORLD YWCA	Natalie Fisher	WORLD YWCA

North and South Agencies

Innocent Kaseke	Africa Representative
Margaret Mwaura	Africa Representative
Tim Moulds	Christian Aid
Jürgen Reichel	EED (Protestant Association for Co-operation in Development)
Ossi Kuoppala	FinnChurchAid
Jacob Franken	Global Ministries of the Uniting Churches in the Netherlands
Bennet Benjamin	India Representative
Karen Bloomquist	Lutheran World Federation
Israel Batista Guerra	South America Representative
Mireya Baltodano	South America Representative
Klaus Heidel	Werkstatt Ökenomie

Steering Group and Project Administration
(see page 92)

NOTES

1 Poverty and Wealth

1 *Bangladesh, Chile, Colombia, Fiji, Germany, Ghana, Hong Kong, India, Jamaica, Namibia, Nicaragua, Palestine, Philippines, South Korea, Uganda, West Indies.*
2 *Bangladesh, Chile, Colombia, Germany, Ghana, India, Jamaica, Malaysia, Nicaragua, LABOUR.*
3 *Bangladesh, Colombia, Fiji, Germany, Jamaica, Namibia, Nicaragua, Philippines, Russia, South Africa, South Korea, West Indies, LABOUR, UN, WORLD YWCA.*
4 *Bangladesh, Chile, Fiji, Jamaica, Malaysia, Philippines, South Korea.*
5 *Bangladesh, Colombia, Fiji, Germany, Jamaica, Malaysia, Nicaragua, Palestine, WORLD YWCA.*
6 *Bangladesh, Chile, Germany, Ghana, India, Nicaragua, South Korea.*
7 *Bangladesh, Chile, Ghana, Jamaica, Malaysia, Nicaragua, Russia, West Indies, LABOUR, WORLD YWCA.*
8 *Bangladesh, Ghana, Nicaragua, WORLD YWCA.*
9 *India, Namibia, Nicaragua, Philippines.*
10 The words 'church' and 'churches' are often used rather loosely to include the churches individually and ecumenically and their development arms, agencies and organizations at the local, national and international levels; these are the 'churches' the Report is about and to which its proposals are addressed.
11 *Bangladesh, Chile, Fiji, Ghana, India, Jamaica, Nicaragua, Philippines, Russia, South Africa, West Indies.*
12 *Fiji, India, South Africa, UN, WORLD YWCA.*
13 *Bangladesh, Chile, India, Jamaica, Nicaragua, West Indies.*
14 *Bangladesh, Chile, Germany, LABOUR.*

2 Causes

1 *Bangladesh, Colombia, Jamaica, Nicaragua, South Africa, Uganda, LABOUR, UN, WORLD YWCA.*
2 *India, Nicaragua, Philippines, Uganda, West Indies.*
3 *Colombia, Fiji, Ghana, Jamaica, Russia, Uganda.*
4 *Bangladesh, Colombia, Hong Kong, Philippines, West Indies, LABOUR, UN, WORLD YWCA.*
5 *Colombia, Fiji, India, Nicaragua, South Korea, Uganda.*
6 *India, Jamaica, Philippines, Uganda, West Indies, UN.*
7 *India, Malaysia, West Indies, TNCs.*
8 *Colombia, India, Jamaica, Malaysia, Nicaragua, Palestine, South Africa, West Indies.*
9 *Bangladesh, Colombia, Jamaica, Nicaragua, WORLD YWCA.*
10 *Bangladesh, Colombia, Fiji, Ghana, Jamaica, Malaysia, Nicaragua, Philippines, Russia, South Africa, South Korea, Uganda, West Indies, WORLD YWCA.*
11 *Bangladesh, Colombia, India, Nicaragua, Philippines, Uganda, West Indies, LABOUR, TNCs, WORLD YWCA.*
12 *Bangladesh, Ghana, Nicaragua, Uganda, WORLD YWCA.*
13 *Bangladesh, India, Jamaica, South Africa, WORLD YWCA.*

14 *Fiji, Ghana, Jamaica, Philippines, Russia, South Africa, Uganda, West Indies, WORLD YWCA.*
15 *Colombia, Jamaica, Nicaragua, West Indies.*
16 *Fiji, Jamaica, Palestine, South Africa, South Korea, WORLD YWCA.*
17 *Ghana, Jamaica, Malaysia, WORLD YWCA.*
18 *Ghana, Fiji, Jamaica, WORLD YWCA.*
19 *Ghana, Jamaica, Malaysia, Uganda, West Indies.*

3 The Teaching of the Churches

 1 *Fiji, Namibia, South Africa, South Korea, LABOUR.*
 2 *Bangladesh, Fiji, Germany, India, Namibia, Philippines, LABOUR.*
 3 *Bangladesh, Germany, Nicaragua, Philippines, West Indies.*
 4 *Bangladesh, Fiji, Germany, Jamaica, LABOUR, UN.*
 5 *Bangladesh, Colombia, Ghana, Malaysia, Philippines, Uganda.*
 6 *Bangladesh, India, Jamaica, Philippines, South Africa.*
 7 *Bangladesh, Chile, Germany, Ghana, Jamaica.*
 8 See page 82 for a list of the seven constituencies.
 9 *Chile, Germany, Ghana, Hong Kong, Jamaica, Russia, South Africa.*
10 *Fiji, Jamaica, Philippines, South Africa, Uganda.*
11 *Colombia, India, Nicaragua, UN.*

4 Overcoming Poverty

 1 *Bangladesh, Chile, Colombia, Fiji, Germany, Ghana, Hong Kong, India, Jamaica, Malaysia, Namibia, Nicaragua, Palestine, Russia, South Korea, West Indies, WORLD YWCA.*
 2 *Bangladesh, Germany, Ghana, Hong Kong, Malaysia, South Korea, West Indies.*
 3 *Bangladesh, Fiji, Germany, Hong Kong, Nicaragua, Palestine, Russia, West Indies.*
 4 *Colombia, India, Nicaragua, Palestine, Philippines, West Indies, WORLD YWCA.*
 5 *Colombia, Hong Kong, Philippines, WORLD YWCA.*
 6 *Colombia, Ghana, Hong Kong, Uganda, West Indies, WORLD YWCA.*
 7 *Bangladesh* p. 11, *Ghana* p. 14, *Fiji* p. 15.
 8 *Bangladesh, Chile, Colombia, Ghana, India, Nicaragua, Palestine, Russia, West Indies, WORLD YWCA.*
 9 *Bangladesh, Chile, Colombia, Namibia, West Indies, WORLD YWCA.*
10 *Malaysia, Namibia, Russia, West Indies.*
11 *Bangladesh, Germany, India, Namibia, WORLD YWCA.*
12 *Chile, Germany, India, Jamaica, Namibia, Philippines, West Indies, TNCs, WORLD YWCA.*
13 *Colombia, Germany, India, Nicaragua, Philippines, West Indies.*
14 *Bangladesh, Germany, Hong Kong, India, Jamaica, Nicaragua, Philippines.*
15 *Bangladesh, Colombia, Ghana, Nicaragua, Philippines, Uganda, West Indies.*
16 *Colombia, Ghana, Namibia, Nicaragua, Russia.*
17 *Colombia, Hong Kong, Palestine, Russia, South Korea, West Indies.*
18 *Colombia, Germany, India, LABOUR.*
19 *Colombia, Germany, India, Namibia, Nicaragua, West Indies, WORLD YWCA.*
20 *Chile, Colombia, Germany, Ghana, India, Jamaica, South Korea.*
21 *Bangladesh, Colombia, Malaysia, Namibia, South Korea.*
22 *Bangladesh, Ghana, Jamaica, Malaysia, Nicaragua, LABOUR.*
23 *Colombia, Germany, India, Jamaica, West Indies.*

5 The Actions of the Churches

 1 *Chile, Colombia, Fiji, Germany, Ghana, Hong Kong, Jamaica, Nicaragua, Palestine, Philippines, Russia, West Indies.*

2 *Colombia, Germany, Ghana, Fiji, Hong Kong, Nicaragua, Palestine, Russia, South Korea, Uganda, West Indies, LABOUR.*

3 *Colombia, Germany, Ghana, Fiji, Jamaica, Namibia, Nicaragua, Palestine, South Korea, Uganda, West Indies, LABOUR.*

4 *Namibia, Nicaragua, Palestine, Uganda, LABOUR.*

5 *Colombia, Ghana, Nicaragua, South Korea, West Indies, LABOUR.*

6 *Ghana, Nicaragua, South Korea, West Indies.*

7 *Chile, Colombia, Fiji, Germany, Jamaica, Nicaragua, Philippines, Russia, South Korea, LABOUR.*

8 *Fiji, Germany, Uganda, West Indies.*

9 *Fiji, Namibia, Palestine, Russia, Uganda.*

6 Recommendations

1 *Hong Kong, West Indies, WORLD YWCA*; see also *TNCs.*

2 *Bangladesh, Chile, Colombia, Fiji, Germany, India, Jamaica, Malaysia, Namibia, Nicaragua, Palestine, Philippines, Russia, South Africa, South Korea, West Indies, LABOUR, WORLD YWCA.*

3 *Chile, Germany, India, Russia.*

4 *Jamaica, Philippines, LABOUR, TNCs.*

5 *Bangladesh, Chile, Colombia, Fiji, Ghana, India, Jamaica, Malaysia, Namibia, Palestine, Philippines, South Africa, Uganda, LABOUR, TNCs, UN.*

6 *Namibia p. 18; Bangladesh, Colombia, Malaysia, Philippines.*

7 *Chile, Colombia, Jamaica, Malaysia.*

8 *Chile, India, South Africa, LABOUR.*

9 *Colombia, Ghana, Uganda, LABOUR.*

10 *Bangladesh, Colombia, Fiji, Jamaica, Philippines, South Africa, LABOUR.*

11 *Colombia, India, South Africa, Uganda.*

12 *Bangladesh, Ghana, India, Jamaica.*

13 For more details see chapters 5 and 6.

14 *Chile, Colombia, India, Jamaica, Philippines, South Africa, Uganda, LABOUR.*

15 North–South terminology is reasonably accurate here but can easily overlook the realities of globalization and the self-understanding of a country such as Russia.

16 *Bangladesh, Chile, Ghana, Philippines, Russia, South Africa, WORLD YWCA.*

17 *Bangladesh, Philippines, Russia, South Africa.*

18 *Bangladesh, Chile, Colombia, Germany, Ghana, Jamaica, Malaysia, Nicaragua, Russia, South Africa, Uganda.*

19 *Chile, Colombia, Germany, South Africa, LABOUR.*

20 *Colombia, India, Jamaica, LABOUR, TNCs, UN.*

21 *Fiji, Germany, Ghana, Uganda, UN.*

22 *Bangladesh, Chile, Germany, Ghana, India, South Africa, South Korea, LABOUR.*

8 The Story of 'Project 21'

1 See J. de Santa Ana, *Towards a Church of the Poor* (Geneva, WCC Publications, 1979); J. de Santa Ana, *Towards a Church in Solidarity with the Poor* (Geneva, WCC Publications, 1980); Michael Taylor, *Not Angels but Agencies* (Geneva, WCC Publications/London, SCM Press, 1995).

2 Michael Taylor, *Not Angels but Agencies*, chapter 6.

3 Comprising three representatives of APRODEV, one representative each from Latin America, Asia, Africa and the WCC and the Secretary and Director of the Project.

4 *Bangladesh, Chile, Colombia, Fiji, Germany* (building on an existing study process of the German churches), *Ghana, Hong Kong* (China), *India, Jamaica, Malaysia, Namibia, Nicaragua, Palestine, Philippines, Russia, South Africa, South Korea, Uganda, West Indies.*

5 *LITURGY; LABOUR; WORLD YWCA; TNCs; UN.*

Index

advocacy 51–4, 59, 64, 69, 71–2
agencies 52–3
AIDS 41, 72
alliances 59–61, 69, 72–4

capacity building 49
charity 36
children 2, 5
   hunger 15
   labour 7, 38–9
churches 34
   advocacy 52–4
   local 74–6
   as NGOs 61, 73, 85
   recommendations to 58–67
   service provision 49
   views on poverty 25–30
civil society 42–3, 49, 55, 58, 69
corruption
   governmental 19–20
culture 21–2

debt 15–16, 87
disasters 12, 21

Ecumenical Advocacy Alliance 72, 74, 79, 85
education 5, 13, 38–40, 49, 56, 69
environment 48, 68

global economy 14–18, 36, 59, 81, 89–90
governance 12, 18–21, 46, 68, 69

healthcare 15, 41
   access 3
holistic teaching 10, 27, 32–4, 70–1
hope 66
   lack of 5
human rights 44–6, 89

International Monetary Fund (IMF) 15–17, 66, 73, 85

jobs and incomes 15, 39–40, 69

land
   colonialism 12
   monopoly of 20
liberation theology 30–3
local communities 61–2, 64, 66, 69, 74–5

methodology 88
Millennium Goals 74, 77–9, xiv

non-governmental organizations (NGOs) 23, 54, 60–1
   churches as 61, 73, 85

poverty
   basic 1–4, 68–9
   psychological 4–5
   self-perpetuating 5, 23, 41–2
   spiritual 5, 8–9, 10–11, 25–30, 68
power 5–6
projects and programmes 43–4, 50, 62–3, 71–2
Prosperity Gospel 29–30, 35, 69

research 13

services 49–51
social capital 37–8
spiritualizing 25–30, 35, 69
stewardship 33–4
subsidiarity 42

theology 64–5, 76–7
   daily 26–7
   prosperity 29–30
trade 14–18, 62
   agricultural 21

transnational corporations (TNCs) 17, 47–8, 55, 60, 62, 66

United Nations 53, 55, 62, 66, 73, 76, 90
　Development Project 84
　Human Development Index 13

values 47, 66, 70–1
　women 46
violence and conflict 7, 13, 63, 65

wealth 22, 35, 68–9
　banks 23
　excessive 70–1, 76
　features of 8–10
　mistrusted 24

women 35, 42, 63
　blocking 22–3
　educating 39
　human rights 46
　status 5
　vulnerability 6–8
World Bank 15–17, 66, 73, 85
　Development Report 84
World Church Report 74, 78, 84–6
World Church Sunday xiv
World Council of Churches (WCC) 53, 61, 74, 81–2
World Trade Organization (WTO) 16–17, 47, 73, 90
worship and liturgy 55–6, 67, 75–6